Maid Marian

Maid Marian

Thomas Love Peacock

DD BOOKS
Publishers for New Generations

Maid Marian
by Thomas Love Peacock

Price: ₹ 250/-

ISBN: 9789359570471

DD Books
Delhi, India

www.ddbookshub.com
ddsalesglobal@gmail.com

Printed in the Republic of INDIA

Contents

Chapter–I

Now come ye for peace here, or come ye for war?

–Scott

The abbot, in his alb arrayed," stood at the altar in the abbey-chapel of Rubygill, with all his plump, sleek, rosy friars, in goodly lines dispose

d, to solemnise the nuptials of the beautiful Matilda Fitzwater, daughter of the Baron of Arlingford, with the noble Robert Fitz-Ooth, Earl of Locksley and Huntingdon. The abbey of Rubygill stood in a picturesque valley, at a little distance from the western boundary of Sherwood Forest, in a spot which seemed adapted by nature to be the retreat of monastic mortification, being on the banks of a fine trout-stream, and in the midst of woodland coverts, abounding with excellent game. The bride, with her father and attendant maidens, entered the chapel; but the earl had not arrived. The baron was amazed, and the bridemaidens were disconcerted. Matilda feared that some evil had befallen her lover, but felt no diminution of her confidence in his honour and love. Through the open gates of the chapel she looked down the narrow road that wound along the side of the hill; and her ear was the first that heard the distant trampling of horses, and her eye was the first that caught the glitter of snowy plumes, and the light of polished spears. "It is strange," thought the baron, "that the earl should come in this martial array to his wedding;" but he had not long to meditate on the phenomenon, for the foaming steeds swept up to the gate like a whirlwind, and the earl, breathless with speed, and followed by a few of his yeomen, advanced to his smiling bride. It was then no time to ask questions, for the organ was in full peal, and the choristers were in full voice.

The abbot began to intone the ceremony in a style of modulation impressively exalted, his voice issuing most canonically from the roof of his mouth, through the medium of a very musical nose newly tuned for the occasion. But he had not proceeded far enough to exhibit all the variety and compass of this melodious instrument, when a noise was heard at the gate, and a party of armed men entered the chapel. The song of the choristers died away in a shake of demisemiquavers, contrary to all the rules of psalmody. The organ-blower, who was working his musical air-pump with one hand, and with two fingers and a thumb of the other insinuating a peeping-place through the curtain of the organ-gallery, was struck motionless by the double operation of curiosity and fear; while the organist, intent only on his performance, and spreading all his fingers to strike a swell of magnificent chords, felt his harmonic spirit ready to desert his body on being answered by the ghastly rattle of empty keys, and in the consequent agitato furioso of the internal movements of his feelings, was preparing to restore harmony by the segue subito of an appoggiatura con foco with the corner of a book of anthems on the head of his neglectful assistant, when his hand and his attention together were arrested by the scene below. The voice of the abbot subsided into silence through a descending scale of long-drawn melody, like the sound of the ebbing sea to the explorers of a cave. In a few moments all was silence, interrupted only by the iron tread of the armed intruders, as it rang on the marble floor and echoed from the vaulted aisles.

The leader strode up to the altar; and placing himself opposite to the abbot, and between the earl and Matilda, in such a manner that the four together seemed to stand on the four points of a diamond, exclaimed, "In the name of King Henry, I forbid the ceremony, and attach Robert Earl of Huntingdon as a traitor!" and at the same time he held his drawn sword between the lovers, as if to emblem that royal authority which laid its temporal ban upon their contract. The earl drew his own sword instantly, and struck down the interposing weapon; then clasped his left arm round Matilda, who sprang into his embrace, and held his sword before her with his right hand. His yeomen ranged themselves at his side, and stood with their swords drawn, still and prepared, like men determined to die in his defence. The soldiers, confident in superiority of numbers, paused. The abbot took advantage of the pause to introduce a word of exhortation. "My children," said he, "if you are going to cut each other's throats, I entreat you, in the name of peace and charity, to do it out of the chapel."

"Sweet Matilda," said the earl, "did you give your love to the Earl of Huntingdon, whose lands touch the Ouse and the Trent, or to Robert Fitz-Ooth, the son of his mother?"

"Neither to the earl nor his earldom," answered Matilda firmly, "but to Robert Fitz-Ooth and his love."

"That I well knew," said the earl; "and though the ceremony be incomplete, we are not the less married in the eye of my only saint, our Lady, who will yet bring us together. Lord Fitzwater, to your care, for the present, I commit your daughter.—Nay, sweet Matilda, part we must for a while; but we will soon meet under brighter skies, and be this the seal of our faith."

He kissed Matilda's lips, and consigned her to the baron, who glowered about him with an expression of countenance that showed he was mortally wroth with somebody; but whatever he thought or felt he kept to himself. The earl, with a sign to his followers, made a sudden charge on the soldiers, with the intention of cutting his way through. The soldiers were prepared for such an occurrence, and a desperate skirmish succeeded.

Some of the women screamed, but none of them fainted; for fainting was not so much the fashion in those days, when the ladies breakfasted on brawn and ale at sunrise, as in our more refined age of green tea and muffins at noon. Matilda seemed disposed to fly again to her lover, but the baron forced her from the chapel. The earl's bowmen at the door sent in among the assailants a volley of arrows, one of which whizzed past the ear of the abbot, who, in mortal fear of being suddenly translated from a ghostly friar into a friarly ghost, began to roll out of the chapel as fast as his bulk and his holy robes would permit, roaring "Sacrilege!" with all his monks at his heels, who were, like himself, more intent to go at once than to stand upon the order of their going. The abbot, thus pressed from behind, and stumbling over his own drapery before, fell suddenly prostrate in the door-way that connected the chapel with the abbey, and was instantaneously buried under a pyramid of ghostly carcasses, that fell over him and each other, and lay a rolling chaos of animated rotundities, sprawling and bawling in unseemly disarray, and sending forth the names of all the saints in and out of heaven, amidst the clashing of swords, the ringing of bucklers, the clattering of helmets, the twanging of bow-strings, the whizzing of arrows, the screams of women, the shouts of the warriors, and the vociferations of the peasantry, who had been assembled to the intended nuptials, and who, seeing a fair set-to, contrived to pick a quarrel among themselves on the occasion, and proceeded, with staff and cudgel, to crack each other's skulls for the good of the king and the earl. One tall friar alone was untouched by the panic of his brethren, and stood steadfastly watching the combat with his arms a-kembo, the colossal emblem of an unarmed neutrality.

At length, through the midst of the internal confusion, the earl, by the help of his good sword, the staunch valour of his men, and the blessing of the Virgin, fought his way to the chapel-gate—his bowmen closed him in—he vaulted into his saddle, clapped spurs to his horse, rallied his men on the first eminence, and exchanged his sword for a bow and arrow, with which he did old execution among the pursuers, who at last thought it most expedient to desist from offensive warfare, and to retreat into the abbey, where, in the king's name, they broached a pipe of the best wine, and attached all the venison in the larder, having first carefully unpacked the tuft of friars, and set the fallen abbot on his legs.

The friars, it may be well supposed, and such of the king's men as escaped unhurt from the affray, found their spirits a cup too low, and kept the flask moving from noon till night. The peaceful brethren, unused to the tumult of war, had undergone, from fear and discomposure, an exhaustion of animal spirits that required extraordinary refection. During the repast, they interrogated Sir Ralph Montfaucon, the leader of the soldiers, respecting the nature of the earl's offence.

"A complication of offences," replied Sir Ralph, "superinduced on the original basis of forest-treason. He began with hunting the king's deer, in despite of all remonstrance; followed it up by contempt of the king's mandates, and by armed resistance to his power, in defiance of all authority; and combined with it the resolute withholding of payment of certain moneys to the abbot of Doncaster, in denial of all law; and has thus made himself the declared enemy of church and state, and all for being too fond of venison." And the knight helped himself to half a pasty.

"A heinous offender," said a little round oily friar, appropriating the portion of pasty which Sir Ralph had left.

"The earl is a worthy peer," said the tall friar whom we have already mentioned in the chapel scene, "and the best marksman in England."

"Why this is flat treason, brother Michael," said the little round friar, "to call an attainted traitor a worthy peer."

"I pledge you," said brother Michael. The little friar smiled and filled his cup. "He will draw the long bow," pursued brother Michael, "with any bold yeoman among them all."

"Don't talk of the long bow," said the abbot, who had the sound of the arrow still whizzing in his ear: "what have we pillars of the faith to do with the long bow?"

"Be that as it may," said Sir Ralph, "he is an outlaw from this moment."

"So much the worse for the law then," said brother Michael. "The law will have a heavier miss of him than he will have of the law. He will strike as much venison as ever, and more of other game. I know what I say: but basta: Let us drink."

"What other game?" said the little friar. "I hope he won't poach among our partridges."

"Poach! not he," said brother Michael: "if he wants your partridges, he will strike them under your nose (here's to you), and drag your trout-stream for you on a Thursday evening."

"Monstrous! and starve us on fast-day," said the little friar.

"But that is not the game I mean," said brother Michael.

"Surely, son Michael," said the abbot, "you do not mean to insinuate that the noble earl will turn freebooter?"

"A man must live," said brother Michael, "earl or no. If the law takes his rents and beeves without his consent, he must take beeves and rents where he can get them without the consent of the law. This is the lex talionis."

"Truly," said Sir Ralph, "I am sorry for the damsel: she seems fond of this wild runagate."

"A mad girl, a mad girl," said the little friar.

"How a mad girl?" said brother Michael. "Has she not beauty, grace, wit, sense, discretion, dexterity, learning, and valour?"

"Learning!" exclaimed the little friar; "what has a woman to do with learning? And valour! who ever heard a woman commended for valour? Meekness and mildness, and softness, and gentleness, and tenderness, and humility, and obedience to her husband, and faith in her confessor, and domesticity, or, as learned doctors call it, the faculty of stayathomeitiveness, and embroidery, and music, and pickling, and preserving, and the whole complex and multiplex detail of the noble science of dinner, as well in preparation for the table, as in arrangement over it, and in distribution around it to knights, and squires, and ghostly friars,—these are female virtues: but valour—why who ever heard—?"

"She is the all in all," said brother Michael, "gentle as a ring-dove, yet high-soaring as a falcon: humble below her deserving, yet deserving beyond the estimate of panegyric: an exact economist in all superfluity, yet a most bountiful dispenser in all liberality: the chief regulator of her household, the fairest pillar of her hall, and the sweetest blossom of her bower: having, in all opposite proposings, sense to understand, judgment to weigh, discretion to choose, firmness to undertake, diligence to conduct, perseverance to accomplish, and resolution to maintain. For obedience to her husband, that is not to be tried till she has one: for faith in her confessor, she has as much as the law prescribes: for embroidery an Arachne: for music a Siren: and for pickling and preserving, did not one of her jars of sugared apricots give you your last surfeit at Arlingford Castle?"

"Call you that preserving?" said the little friar; "I call it destroying. Call you it pickling? Truly it pickled me. My life was saved by miracle."

"By canary," said brother Michael. "Canary is the only life preserver, the true aurum potabile, the universal panacea for all diseases, thirst, and short life. Your life was saved by canary."

"Indeed, reverend father," said Sir Ralph, "if the young lady be half what you describe, she must be a paragon: but your commending her for valour does somewhat amaze me."

"She can fence," said the little friar, "and draw the long bow, and play at singlestick and quarter-staff."

"Yet mark you," said brother Michael, "not like a virago or a hoyden, or one that would crack a serving-man's head for spilling gravy on her ruff, but with such womanly grace and temperate self-command as if those manly exercises belonged to her only, and were become for her sake feminine."

"You incite me," said Sir Ralph, "to view her more nearly. That madcap earl found me other employment than to remark her in the chapel."

"The earl is a worthy peer," said brother Michael; "he is worth any fourteen earls on this side Trent, and any seven on the other." (The reader will please to remember that Rubygill Abbey was north of Trent.)

"His mettle will be tried," said Sir Ralph. "There is many a courtier will swear to King Henry to bring him in dead or alive."

"They must look to the brambles then," said brother Michael.

"The bramble, the bramble, the bonny forest bramble,
Doth make a jest
Of silken vest,
That will through greenwood scramble
The bramble, the bramble, the bonny forest bramble"

"Plague on your lungs, son Michael," said the abbot; "this is your old coil: always roaring in your cups."

"I know what I say," said brother Michael; "there is often more sense in an old song than in a new homily.

The courtly pad doth amble,
When his gay lord would ramble:
ut both may catch
An awkward scratch,
If they ride among the bramble
The bramble, the bramble, the bonny forest bramble"

"Tall friar," said Sir Ralph, "either you shoot the shafts of your merriment at random, or you know more of the earl's designs than beseems your frock."

"Let my frock," said brother Michael, "answer for its own sins. It is worn past covering mine. It is too weak for a shield, too transparent for a screen, too thin for a shelter, too light for gravity, and too threadbare for a jest. The wearer would be naught indeed who should misbeseem such a wedding garment.

But wherefore does the sheep wear wool?
That he in season sheared may be,
And the shepherd be warm though his flock be cool:
So I'll have a new cloak about me."

❖❖❖

Chapter–II

Vray moyne si oncques en feut depuis que
le monde moynantmoyna de moynerie

–Rabelais

The Earl of Huntingdon, living in the vicinity of a royal forest, and passionately attached to the chase from his infancy, had long made as free with the king's deer as Lord Percy proposed to do with those of Lord Douglas in the memorable hunting of Cheviot. It is sufficiently well known how severe were the forest-laws in those days, and with what jealousy the kings of England maintained this branch of their prerogative; but menaces and remonstrances were thrown away on the earl, who declared that he would not thank Saint Peter for admission into Paradise, if he were obliged to leave his bow and hounds at the gate. King Henry (the Second) swore by Saint Botolph to make him rue his sport, and, having caused him to be duly and formally accused, summoned him to London to answer the charge. The earl, deeming himself safer among his own vassals than among king Henry's courtiers, took no notice of the mandate. King Henry sent a force to bring him, vi et armis, to court. The earl made a resolute resistance, and put the king's force to flight under a shower of arrows: an act which the courtiers declared to be treason. At the same time, the abbot of Doncaster sued up the payment of certain moneys, which the earl, whose revenue ran a losing race with his hospitality, had borrowed at sundry times of the said abbot: for the abbots and the bishops were the chief usurers of those days, and, as the end sanctifies the means, were not in the least scrupulous of employing what would have been extortion in the profane, to accomplish the pious purpose of bringing a blessing on the land by rescuing it from the frail hold of carnal and temporal into the firmer grasp of ghostly and spiritual possessors. But the earl, confident in the number and attachment of his retainers, stoutly refused either to repay the money, which he could not, or to yield the forfeiture, which he would not: a refusal which in those days was an act of outlawry in a gentleman, as it is now of bankruptcy in a base mechanic; the gentleman having in our wiser times a more liberal privilege of gentility, which enables him to keep his land and laugh at his creditor. Thus the mutual resentments and interests of the king and the abbot concurred to subject the earl to the penalties of outlawry, by which the abbot would gain his due upon the lands of Locksley, and the rest would be confiscate to the king. Still the king did not think it advisable to assail the earl in his own strong-hold, but caused a diligent watch to be kept over his motions, till at length his rumoured marriage with the heiress of Arlingford seemed to point out an easy method of laying violent hands on the offender. Sir Ralph Montfaucon, a young man of good lineage and of an aspiring temper, who readily seized the first opportunity that offered of recommending himself to King Henry's favour by manifesting his zeal in his service, undertook the charge: and how he succeeded we have seen.

Sir Ralph's curiosity was strongly excited by the friar's description of the young lady of Arlingford; and he prepared in the morning to visit the castle, under the very plausible pretext of giving the baron an explanation of his intervention at the nuptials. Brother Michael and the little fat friar proposed to be his guides. The proposal was courteously accepted, and they set out together, leaving Sir Ralph's followers at the abbey. The knight was mounted on a spirited charger; brother Michael on a large heavy-trotting horse; and the little fat friar on a plump soft-paced galloway, so correspondent with himself in size, rotundity, and sleekness, that if they had been amalgamated into a centaur, there would have been nothing to alter in their proportions.

"Do you know," said the little friar, as they wound along the banks of the stream, "the reason why lake-trout is better than river-trout, and shyer withal?"

"I was not aware of the fact," said Sir Ralph.

"A most heterodox remark," said brother Michael: "know you not, that in all nice matters you should take the implication for absolute, and, without looking into the FACT WHETHER, seek only the reason why? But the fact is so, on the word of a friar; which what layman will venture to gainsay who prefers a down bed to a gridiron?"

"The fact being so," said the knight, "I am still at a loss for the reason; nor would I undertake to opine in a matter of that magnitude: since, in all that appertains to the good things either of this world or the next, my reverend spiritual guides are kind enough to take the trouble of thinking off my hands."

"Spoken," said brother Michael, "with a sound Catholic conscience. My little brother here is most profound in the matter of trout. He has marked, learned, and inwardly digested the subject, twice a week at least for five-and-thirty years. I yield to him in this. My strong points are venison and canary."

"The good qualities of a trout," said the little friar, "are firmness and redness: the redness, indeed, being the visible sign of all other virtues."

"Whence," said brother Michael, "we choose our abbot by his nose:

The rose on the nose doth all virtues disclose:
For the outward grace shows

That the inward overflows,
When it glows in the rose of a red, red nose."

"Now," said the little friar, "as is the firmness so is the redness, and as is the redness so is the shyness."

"Marry why?" said brother Michael. "The solution is not physical-natural, but physical-historical, or natural-superinductive. And thereby hangs a tale, which may be either said or sung:

The damsel stood to watch the fight
By the banks of Kingslea Mere,
And they brought to her feet her own true knight
Sore-wounded on a bier.

She knelt by him his wounds to bind,
She washed them with many a tear:
And shouts rose fast upon the wind,
Which told that the foe was near.

"Oh! let not," he said, "while yet I live,
The cruel foe me take:
But with thy sweet lips a last kiss give,
And cast me in the lake."

Around his neck she wound her arms,
And she kissed his lips so pale:
And evermore the war's alarms
Came louder up the vale.

She drew him to the lake's steep side,
Where the red heath fringed the shore;
She plunged with him beneath the tide,
And they were seen no more.

Their true blood mingled in Kingslea Mere,
That to mingle on earth was fain:

And the trout that swims in that crystal clear
Is tinged with the crimson stain

"Thus you see how good comes of evil, and how a holy friar may fare better on fast-day for the violent death of two lovers two hundred years ago. The inference is most consecutive, that wherever you catch a red-fleshed trout, love lies bleeding under the water: an occult quality, which can only act in the stationary waters of a lake, being neutralised by the rapid transition of those of a stream."

"And why is the trout shyer for that?" asked Sir Ralph.

"Do you not see?" said brother Michael. "The virtues of both lovers diffuse themselves through the lake. The infusion of masculine valour makes the fish active and sanguineous: the infusion of maiden modesty makes him coy and hard to win: and you shall find through life, the fish which is most easily hooked is not the best worth dishing. But yonder are the towers of Arlingford."

The little friar stopped. He seemed suddenly struck with an awful thought, which caused a momentary pallescence in his rosy complexion; and after a brief hesitation, he turned his galloway, and told his companions he should give them good day.

"Why, what is in the wind now, brother Peter?" said Friar Michael.

"The lady Matilda," said the little friar, "can draw the long-bow. She must bear no goodwill to Sir Ralph; and if she should espy him from her tower, she may testify her recognition with a cloth-yard shaft. She is not so infallible a markswoman, but that she might shoot at a crow and kill a pigeon. She might peradventure miss the knight, and hit me, who never did her any harm."

"Tut, tut, man," said brother Michael, "there is no such fear."

"Mass," said the little friar, "but there is such a fear, and very strong too. You who have it not may keep your way, and I who have it shall take mine. I am not just now in the vein for being picked off at a long shot." And saying these words, he spurred up his four-footed better half, and galloped off as nimbly as if he had had an arrow singing behind him.

"Is this lady Matilda, then, so very terrible a damsel?" said Sir Ralph to brother Michael.

"By no means," said the friar. "She has certainly a high spirit; but it is the wing of the eagle, without his beak or his claw. She is as gentle as magnanimous; but it is the gentleness of the summer wind, which, however lightly it wave the tuft of the pine, carries with it the intimation of a power, that, if roused to its extremity, could make it bend to the dust."

"From the warmth of your panegyric, ghostly father," said the knight, "I should almost suspect you were in love with the damsel."

"So I am," said the friar, "and I care not who knows it; but all in the way of honesty, master soldier. I am, as it were, her spiritual lover; and were she a damsel errant, I would be her ghostly esquire, her friar militant. I would buckle me in armour of proof, and the devil might thresh me black with an iron flail, before I would knock under in her cause. Though they be not yet one canonically, thanks to your soldiership, the earl is her liege lord, and she is his liege lady. I am her father confessor and ghostly director: I have taken on me to show her the way to the next world; and how can I do that if I lose sight of her in this? seeing that this is but the road to the other, and has so many circumvolutions and ramifications of byeways and beaten paths (all more thickly set than the true one with finger-posts and milestones, not one of which tells truth), that a traveller has need of some one who knows the way, or the odds go hard against him that he will ever see the face of Saint Peter."

"But there must surely be some reason," said Sir Ralph, "for father Peter's apprehension."

"None," said brother Michael, "but the apprehension itself; fear being its own father, and most prolific in self-propagation. The lady did, it is true, once signalize her displeasure against our little brother, for reprimanding her in that she would go hunting a-mornings instead of attending matins. She cut short the thread of his eloquence by sportively drawing her bow-string and loosing an arrow over his head; he waddled off with singular speed, and was in much awe of her for many months. I thought he had forgotten it: but let that pass. In truth, she would have had little of her lover's company, if she had liked the chaunt of the choristers better than the cry of the hounds: yet I know not; for they were companions from the cradle, and reciprocally fashioned each other to the love of the fern and the foxglove. Had either been less sylvan, the other might have been more saintly; but they will now never hear matins but those of the lark, nor reverence vaulted aisle but that of the greenwood canopy. They are twin plants of the forest, and are identified with its growth.

For the slender beech and the sapling oak,
That grow by the shadowy rill,
You may cut down both at a single stroke,
You may cut down which you will.

But this you must know, that as long as they grow
Whatever change may be,
You never can teach either oak or beech
To be aught but a greenwood tree."

❖❖❖

Chapter–III

Inflamed wrath in glowing breast

–Butler

The knight and the friar arriving at Arlingford Castle, and leaving their horses in the care of lady Matilda's groom, with whom the friar was in great favour, were ushered into a stately apartment, where they found the baron alone, flourishing an enormous carving-knife over a brother baron—of beef—with as much vehemence of action as if he were cutting down an enemy. The baron was a gentleman of a fierce and choleric temperament: he was lineally descended from the redoubtable Fierabras of Normandy, who came over to England with the Conqueror, and who, in the battle of Hastings, killed with his own hand four-and-twenty Saxon cavaliers all on a row. The very excess of the baron's internal rage on the preceding day had smothered its external manifestation: he was so equally angry with both parties, that he knew not on which to vent his wrath. He was enraged with the earl for having brought himself into such a dilemma without his privily; and he was no less enraged with the king's men for their very unseasonable intrusion. He could willingly have fallen upon both parties, but, he must necessarily have begun with one; and he felt that on whichever side he should strike the first blow, his retainers would immediately join battle. He had therefore contented himself with forcing away his daughter from the scene of action. In the course of the evening he had received intelligence that the earl's castle was in possession of a party of the king's men, who had been detached by Sir Ralph Montfaucon to seize on it during the earl's absence. The baron inferred from this that the earl's case was desperate; and those who have had the opportunity of seeing a rich friend fall suddenly into poverty, may easily judge by their own feelings how quickly and completely the whole moral being of the earl was changed in the baron's estimation. The baron immediately proceeded to require in his daughter's mind the same summary revolution that had taken place in his own, and considered himself exceedingly ill-used by her non-compliance. The lady had retired to her chamber, and the baron had passed a supperless and sleepless night, stalking about his apartments till an advanced hour of the morning, when hunger compelled him to summon into his presence the spoils of the buttery, which, being the intended array of an uneaten wedding feast, were more than usually abundant, and on which, when the knight and the friar entered, he was falling with desperate valour. He looked up at them fiercely, with his mouth full of beef and his eyes full of flame, and rising, as ceremony required, made an awful bow to the knight, inclining himself forward over the table and presenting his carving-knife en militaire, in a manner that seemed to leave it doubtful whether he meant to show respect to his visitor, or to defend his provision: but the doubt was soon cleared up by his politely motioning the knight to be seated; on which the friar advanced to the table, saying, "For what we are going to receive," and commenced operations without further prelude by filling and drinking a goblet of wine. The baron at the same time offered one to Sir Ralph, with the look of a man in whom habitual hospitality and courtesy were struggling with the ebullitions of natural anger. They pledged each other in silence, and the baron, having completed a copious draught, continued working his lips and his throat, as if trying to swallow his wrath as he had done his wine. Sir Ralph, not knowing well what to make of these ambiguous signs, looked for instructions to the friar, who by significant looks and gestures seemed to advise him to follow his example and partake of the good cheer before him, without speaking till the baron should be more intelligible in his demeanour. The knight and the friar, accordingly, proceeded to refect themselves after their ride; the baron looking first at the one and then at the other, scrutinising alternately the serious looks of the knight and the merry face of the friar, till at length, having calmed himself sufficiently to speak, he said, "Courteous knight and ghostly father, I presume you have some other business with me than to eat my beef and drink my canary; and if so, I patiently await your leisure to enter on the topic."

"Lord Fitzwater," said Sir Ralph, "in obedience to my royal master, King Henry, I have been the unwilling instrument of frustrating the intended nuptials of your fair daughter; yet will you, I trust, owe me no displeasure for my agency herein, seeing that the noble maiden might otherwise by this time have been the bride of an outlaw."

"I am very much obliged to you, sir," said the baron; "very exceedingly obliged. Your solicitude for my daughter is truly paternal, and for a young man and a stranger very singular and exemplary: and it is very kind withal to come to the relief of my insufficiency and inexperience, and concern yourself so much in that which concerns you not."

"You misconceive the knight, noble baron," said the friar. "He urges not his reason in the shape of a preconceived intent, but in that of a subsequent extenuation. True, he has done the lady Matilda great wrong—"

"How, great wrong?" said the baron. "What do you mean by great wrong? Would you have had her married to a wild fly-by-night, that accident made an earl and nature a deer-stealer? that has not wit enough to eat venison without picking a quarrel with monarchy? that flings away his own lands into the clutches of rascally friars, for the sake of hunting in other men's grounds, and feasting vagabonds that wear Lincoln green, and would have flung away mine into the bargain if he had had my daughter? What do you mean by great wrong?"

"True," said the friar, "great right, I meant."

"Right!" exclaimed the baron: "what right has any man to do my daughter right but myself? What right has any man to drive my daughter's bridegroom out of the chapel in the middle of the marriage ceremony, and turn all our merry faces into green wounds and bloody coxcombs, and then come and tell me he has done us great right?"

"True," said the friar: "he has done neither right nor wrong."

"But he has," said the baron, "he has done both, and I will maintain it with my glove."

"It shall not need," said Sir Ralph; "I will concede any thing in honour."

"And I," said the baron, "will concede nothing in honour: I will concede nothing in honour to any man."

"Neither will I, Lord Fitzwater," said Sir Ralph, "in that sense: but hear me. I was commissioned by the king to apprehend the Earl of Huntingdon. I brought with me a party of soldiers, picked and tried men, knowing that he would not lightly yield. I sent my lieutenant with a detachment to surprise the earl's castle in his absence, and laid my measures for intercepting him on the way to his intended nuptials; but he seems to have had intimation of this part of my plan, for he brought with him a large armed retinue, and took a circuitous route, which made him, I believe, somewhat later than his appointed hour. When the lapse of time showed me that he had taken another track, I pursued him to the chapel; and I would have awaited the close of the ceremony, if I had thought that either yourself or your daughter would have felt desirous that she should have been the bride of an outlaw."

"Who said, sir," cried the baron, "that we were desirous of any such thing? But truly, sir, if I had a mind to the devil for a son-in-law, I would fain see the man that should venture to interfere."

"That would I," said the friar; "for I have undertaken to make her renounce the devil."

"She shall not renounce the devil," said the baron, "unless I please. You are very ready with your undertakings. Will you undertake to make her renounce the earl, who, I believe, is the devil incarnate? Will you undertake that?"

"Will I undertake," said the friar, "to make Trent run westward, or to make flame burn downward, or to make a tree grow with its head in the earth and its root in the air?"

"So then," said the baron, "a girl's mind is as hard to change as nature and the elements, and it is easier to make her renounce the devil than a lover. Are you a match for the devil, and no match for a man?"

"My warfare," said the friar, "is not of this world. I am militant not against man, but the devil, who goes about seeking what he may devour."

"Oh! does he so?" said the baron: "then I take it that makes you look for him so often in my buttery. Will you cast out the devil whose name is Legion, when you cannot cast out the imp whose name is Love?"

"Marriages," said the friar, "are made in heaven. Love is God's work, and therewith I meddle not."

"God's work, indeed!" said the baron, "when the ceremony was cut short in the church. Could men have put them asunder, if God had joined them together? And the earl is now no earl, but plain Robert Fitz-Ooth: therefore, I'll none of him."

"He may atone," said the friar, "and the king may mollify. The earl is a worthy peer, and the king is a courteous king."

"He cannot atone," said Sir Ralph. "He has killed the king's men; and if the baron should aid and abet, he will lose his castle and land."

"Will I?" said the baron; "not while I have a drop of blood in my veins. He that comes to take them shall first serve me as the friar serves my flasks of canary: he shall drain me dry as hay. Am I not disparaged? Am I not outraged? Is not my daughter vilified, and made a mockery? A girl half-married? There was my butler brought home with a broken head. My butler, friar: there is that may move your sympathy. Friar, the earl-no-earl shall come no more to my daughter."

"Very good," said the friar.

"It is not very good," said the baron, "for I cannot get her to say so."

"I fear," said Sir Ralph, "the young lady must be much distressed and discomposed."

"Not a whit, sir," said the baron. "She is, as usual, in a most provoking imperturbability, and contradicts me so smilingly that it would enrage you to see her."

"I had hoped," said Sir Ralph, "that I might have seen her, to make my excuse in person for the hard necessity of my duty."

He had scarcely spoken, when the door opened, and the lady made her appearance.

❖❖❖

Chapter–IV

Are you mad, or what are you, that you squeak out your catches without mitigation or remorse of voice?

– Twelfth Night

Matilda, not dreaming of visitors, tripped into the apartment in a dress of forest green, with a small quiver by her side, and a bow and arrow in her hand. Her hair, black and glossy as the raven's wing, curled like wandering clusters of dark ripe grapes under the edge of her round bonnet; and a plume of black feathers fell back negligently above it, with an almost horizontal inclination, that seemed the habitual effect of rapid motion against the wind. Her black eyes sparkled like sunbeams on a river: a clear, deep, liquid radiance, the reflection of ethereal fire,—tempered, not subdued, in the medium of its living and gentle mirror. Her lips were half opened to speak as she entered the apartment; and with a smile of recognition to the friar, and a courtesy to the stranger knight, she approached the baron and said, "You are late at your breakfast, father."

"I am not at breakfast," said the baron. "I have been at supper: my last night's supper; for I had none."

"I am sorry," said Matilda, "you should have gone to bed supperless."

"I did not go to bed supperless," said the baron: "I did not go to bed at all: and what are you doing with that green dress and that bow and arrow?"

"I am going a-hunting," said Matilda.

"A-hunting!" said the baron. "What, I warrant you, to meet with the earl, and slip your neck into the same noose?"

"No," said Matilda: "I am not going out of our own woods to-day."

"How do I know that?" said the baron. "What surety have I of that?"

"Here is the friar," said Matilda. "He will be surety."

"Not he," said the baron: "he will undertake nothing but where the devil is a party concerned."

"Yes, I will," said the friar: "I will undertake any thing for the lady Matilda."

"No matter for that," said the baron: "she shall not go hunting to day."

"Why, father," said Matilda, "if you coop me up here in this odious castle, I shall pine and die like a lonely swan on a pool.

"No," said the baron, "the lonely swan does not die on the pool. If there be a river at hand, she flies to the river, and finds her a mate; and so shall not you."

"But," said Matilda, "you may send with me any, or as many, of your grooms as you will."

"My grooms," said the baron, "are all false knaves. There is not a rascal among them but loves you better than me. Villains that I feed and clothe."

"Surely," said Matilda, "it is not villany to love me: if it be, I should be sorry my father were an honest man." The baron relaxed his muscles into a smile. "Or my lover either," added Matilda. The baron looked grim again.

"For your lover," said the baron, "you may give God thanks of him. He is as arrant a knave as ever poached."

"What, for hunting the king's deer?" said Matilda. "Have I not heard you rail at the forest laws by the hour?"

"Did you ever hear me," said the baron, "rail myself out of house and land? If I had done that, then were I a knave."

"My lover," said Matilda, "is a brave man, and a true man, and a generous man, and a young man, and a handsome man; aye, and an honest man too."

"How can he be an honest man," said the baron, "when he has neither house nor land, which are the better part of a man?"

"They are but the husk of a man," said Matilda, "the worthless coat of the chesnut: the man himself is the kernel."

"The man is the grape stone," said the baron, "and the pulp of the melon. The house and land are the true substantial fruit, and all that give him savour and value."

"He will never want house or land," said Matilda, "while the meeting boughs weave a green roof in the wood, and the free range of the hart marks out the bounds of the forest."

"Vert and venison! vert and venison!" exclaimed the baron. "Treason and flat rebellion. Confound your smiling face! what makes you look so good-humoured? What! you think I can't look at you, and be in a passion? You think so, do you? We shall see. Have you no fear in talking thus, when here is the king's liegeman come to take us all into custody, and confiscate our goods and chattels?"

"Nay, Lord Fitzwater," said Sir Ralph, "you wrong me in your report. My visit is one of courtesy and excuse, not of menace and authority."

"There it is," said the baron: "every one takes a pleasure in contradicting me. Here is this courteous knight, who has not opened his mouth three times since he has been in my house except to take in provision, cuts me short in my story with a flat denial."

"Oh! I cry you mercy, sir knight," said Matilda; "I did not mark you before. I am your debtor for no slight favour, and so is my liege lord."

"Her liege lord!" exclaimed the baron, taking large strides across the chamber.

"Pardon me, gentle lady," said Sir Ralph. "Had I known you before yesterday, I would have cut off my right hand ere it should have been raised to do you displeasure.

"Oh sir," said Matilda, "a good man may be forced on an ill office: but I can distinguish the man from his duty." She presented to him her hand, which he kissed respectfully, and simultaneously with the contact thirty-two invisible arrows plunged at once into his heart, one from every point of the compass of his pericardia.

"Well, father," added Matilda, "I must go to the woods."

"Must you?" said the baron; "I say you must not."

"But I am going," said Matilda

"But I will have up the drawbridge," said the baron.

"But I will swim the moat," said Matilda.

"But I will secure the gates," said the baron.

"But I will leap from the battlement," said Matilda.

"But I will lock you in an upper chamber," said the baron.

"But I will shred the tapestry," said Matilda, "and let myself down."

"But I will lock you in a turret," said the baron, "where you shall only see light through a loophole."

"But through that loophole," said Matilda, "will I take my flight, like a young eagle from its eerie; and, father, while I go out freely, I will return willingly: but if once I slip out through a loop-hole—" She paused a moment, and then added, singing,—

The love that follows fain
Will never its faith betray:
But the faith that is held in a chain
Will never be found again,
If a single link give way.

The melody acted irresistibly on the harmonious propensities of the friar, who accordingly sang in his turn,—

For hark! hark! hark!
The dog doth bark,
The hunter awakes at the peep of the dawn,
But the lair it is empty, the deer it is gone,
And the hunter knows not where.

Matilda and the friar then sang together,—

Then follow, oh follow! the hounds do cry:
The red sun flames in the eastern sky:
The stag bounds over the hollow.
He that lingers in spirit, or loiters in hall,
Shall see us no more till the evening fall,
And no voice but the echo shall answer his call:
Then follow, oh follow, follow:
Follow, oh follow, follow!

During the process of this harmony, the baron's eyes wandered from his daughter to the friar, and from the friar to his daughter again, with an alternate expression of anger differently modified: when he looked on the friar, it was anger without qualification; when he looked on his daughter it was still anger, but tempered by an expression of involuntary admiration and pleasure. These rapid fluctuations of the baron's physiognomy—the habitual, reckless, resolute merriment in the jovial face of the friar,—and the cheerful, elastic spirits that played on the lips and sparkled in the eyes of Matilda,—would have presented a very amusing combination to Sir Ralph, if one of the three images in the group had not absorbed his total attention with feelings of intense delight very nearly allied to pain. The baron's wrath was somewhat counteracted by the reflection that his daughter's good spirits seemed to show that they would naturally rise triumphant over all disappointments; and he had had sufficient experience of her humour to know that she might sometimes be led, but never could be driven. Then, too, he was always delighted to hear her sing, though he was not at all pleased in this instance with the subject of her song. Still he would have endured the subject for the sake of the melody of the treble, but his mind was not sufficiently attuned to unison to relish the harmony of the bass. The friar's accompaniment put him out of all patience, and—"So," he exclaimed, "this is the way, you teach my daughter to renounce the devil, is it? A hunting friar, truly! Who ever heard before of a hunting friar? A profane, roaring, bawling, bumper-bibbing, neck-breaking, catch-singing friar?"

"Under favour, bold baron," said the friar; but the friar was warm with canary, and in his singing vein; and he could not go on in plain unmusical prose. He therefore sang in a new tune,—

Though I be now a grey, grey friar,
Yet I was once a hale young knight:
The cry of my dogs was the only choir
In which my spirit did take delight.
Little I recked of matin bell,
But drowned its toll with my clanging horn:
And the only beads I loved to tell
Were the beads of dew on the spangled thorn.

The baron was going to storm, but the friar paused, and Matilda sang in repetition,—

Little I reck of matin bell,
But drown its toll with my clanging horn:
And the only beads I love to tell
Are the beads of dew on the spangled thorn.

And then she and the friar sang the four lines together, and rang the changes upon them alternately.

Little I reck of matin bell,

sang the friar.

"A precious friar," said the baron.

But drown its toll with my clanging horn, sang Matilda.

"More shame for you," said the baron.

And the only beads I love to tell
Are the beads of dew on the spangled thorn,

sang Matilda and the friar together.

"Penitent and confessor," said the baron: "a hopeful pair truly."

The friar went on,—

An archer keen I was withal,
As ever did lean on greenwood tree;
And could make the fleetest roebuck fall,
A good three hundred yards from me.
Though changeful time, with hand severe,
Has made me now these joys forego,
Yet my heart bounds whene'er I hear
Yoicks! hark away! and tally ho!

Matilda chimed in as before.

"Are you mad?" said the baron. "Are you insane? Are you possessed? What do you mean? What in the devil's name do you both mean?"

Yoicks! hark away! and tally ho!

roared the friar.

The baron's pent-up wrath had accumulated like the waters above the dam of an overshot mill. The pond-head of his passion being now filled to the utmost limit of its capacity, and beginning to overflow in the quivering of his lips and the flashing of his eyes, he pulled up all the flash-boards at once, and gave loose to the full torrent of his indignation, by seizing, like furious Ajax, not a messy stone more than two modern men could raise, but a vast dish of beef more than fifty ancient yeomen could eat, and whirled it like a coit, in terrorem, over the head of the friar, to the extremity of the apartment,

Where it on oaken floor did settle,
With mighty din of ponderous metal.

"Nay father," said Matilda, taking the baron's hand, "do not harm the friar: he means not to offend you. My gaiety never before displeased you. Least of all should it do so now, when I have need of all my spirits to outweigh the severity of my fortune."

As she spoke the last words, tears started into her eyes, which, as if ashamed of the involuntary betraying of her feelings, she turned away to conceal. The baron was subdued at once. He kissed his daughter, held out his hand to the friar, and said, "Sing on, in God's name, and crack away the flasks till your voice swims in canary." Then turning to Sir Ralph, he said, "You see how it is, sir knight. Matilda is my daughter; but she has me in leading-strings, that is the truth of it."

Chapter–V

T is true, no lover has that power
To enforce a desperate amour
As he that has two strings to his bow
And burns for love and money too

–Butler

The friar had often had experience of the baron's testy humour; but it had always before confined itself to words, in which the habit of testiness often mingled more expression of displeasure than the internal feeling prompted. He knew the baron to be hot and choleric, but at the same time hospitable and generous; passionately fond of his daughter, often thwarting her in seeming, but always yielding to her in fact. The early attachment between Matilda and the Earl of Huntingdon had given the baron no serious reason to interfere with her habits and pursuits, which were so congenial to those of her lover; and not being over-burdened with orthodoxy, that is to say, not being seasoned with more of the salt of the spirit than was necessary to preserve him from excommunication, confiscation, and philotheoparoptesism, [1]he was not sorry to encourage his daughter's choice of her confessor in brother Michael, who had more jollity and less hypocrisy than any of his fraternity, and was very little anxious to disguise his love of the good things of this world under the semblance of a sanctified exterior. The friar

---

[1] Roasting by a slow fire for the love of God

and Matilda had often sung duets together, and had been accustomed to the baron's chiming in with a stormy capriccio, which was usually charmed into silence by some sudden turn in the witching melodies of Matilda. They had therefore naturally calculated, as far as their wild spirits calculated at all, on the same effects from the same causes. But the circumstances of the preceding day had made an essential alteration in the case. The baron knew well, from the intelligence he had received, that the earl's offence was past remission: which would have been of less moment but for the awful fact of his castle being in the possession of the king's forces, and in those days possession was considerably more than eleven points of the law. The baron was therefore convinced that the earl's outlawry was infallible, and that Matilda must either renounce her lover, or become with him an outlaw and a fugitive. In proportion, therefore, to the baron's knowledge of the strength and duration of her attachment, was his fear of the difficulty of its ever being overcome: her love of the forest and the chase, which he had never before discouraged, now presented itself to him as matter of serious alarm; and if her cheerfulness gave him hope on the one hand by indicating a spirit superior to all disappointments, it was suspicious to him on the other, as arising from some latent certainty of being soon united to the earl. All these circumstances concurred to render their songs of the vanished deer and greenwood archery and Yoicks and Harkaway, extremely mal-a-propos, and to make his anger boil and bubble in the cauldron of his spirit, till its more than ordinary excitement burst forth with sudden impulse into active manifestation.

But as it sometimes happens, from the might
Of rage in minds that can no farther go,
As high as they have mounted in despite

In their remission do they sink as low,
To our bold baron did it happen so[2]

For his discobolic exploit proved the climax of his rage, and was succeeded by an immediate sense that he had passed the bounds of legitimate passion; and he sunk immediately from the very pinnacle of opposition to the level of implicit acquiescence. The friar's spirits were not to be marred by such a little incident. He was half-inclined, at first, to return the baron's compliment; but his love of Matilda checked him; and when the baron held out his hand, the friar seized it cordially, and they drowned all recollection of the affair by pledging each other in a cup of canary.

The friar, having stayed long enough to see every thing replaced on a friendly footing, rose, and moved to take his leave. Matilda told him he must come again on the morrow, for she had a very long confession to make to him. This the friar promised to do, and departed with the knight.

Sir Ralph, on reaching the abbey, drew his followers together, and led them to Locksley Castle, which he found in the possession of his lieutenant; whom he again left there with a sufficient force to hold it in safe keeping in the king's name, and proceeded to London to report the results of his enterprise.

Now Henry our royal king was very wroth at the earl's evasion, and swore by Saint Thomas-a-Becket (whom he had himself translated into a saint by having him knocked on the head), that he would give the castle and lands of Locksley to the man who should bring in the earl. Hereupon ensued a process of thought in the mind of the knight. The eyes of the fair huntress of Arlingford had left a wound in his heart which only she who

---

[2] Of these lines all that is not in italics belongs to Mr. Wordsworth: Resolution and Independence

gave could heal. He had seen that the baron was no longer very partial to the outlawed earl, but that he still retained his old affection for the lands and castle of Locksley. Now the lands and castle were very fair things in themselves, and would be pretty appurtenances to an adventurous knight; but they would be doubly valuable as certain passports to the father's favour, which was one step towards that of the daughter, or at least towards obtaining possession of her either quietly or perforce; for the knight was not so nice in his love as to consider the lady's free grace a sine qua non: and to think of being, by any means whatever, the lord of Locksley and Arlingford, and the husband of the bewitching Matilda, was to cut in the shades of futurity a vista very tempting to a soldier of fortune. He set out in high spirits with a chosen band of followers, and beat up all the country far and wide around both the Ouse and the Trent; but fortune did not seem disposed to second his diligence, for no vestige whatever could he trace of the earl. His followers, who were only paid with the wages of hope, began to murmur and fall off; for, as those unenlightened days were ignorant of the happy invention of paper machinery, by which one promise to pay is satisfactorily paid with another promise to pay, and that again with another in infinite series, they would not, as their wiser posterity has done, take those tenders for true pay which were not sterling; so that, one fine morning, the knight found himself sitting on a pleasant bank of the Trent, with only a solitary squire, who still clung to the shadow of preferment, because he did not see at the moment any better chance of the substance.

The knight did not despair because of the desertion of his followers: he was well aware that he could easily raise recruits if he could once find trace of his game; he, therefore, rode about indefatigably over hill and dale, to the great sharpening of his own appetite and that of his squire, living gallantly from inn to inn when his purse was full, and quartering himself in the king's name on the nearest ghostly brotherhood when it happened to be empty. An autumn and a winter had passed away, when the course of his perlustations brought him one evening into a beautiful sylvan valley, where he found a number of young women weaving garlands of flowers, and singing over their pleasant occupation. He approached them, and courteously inquired the way to the nearest town.

"There is no town within several miles," was the answer.

"A village, then, if it be but large enough to furnish an inn?"

"There is Gamwell just by, but there is no inn nearer than the nearest town."

"An abbey, then?"

"There is no abbey nearer than the nearest inn."

"A house then, or a cottage, where I may obtain hospitality for the night?"

"Hospitality!" said one of the young women; "you have not far to seek for that. Do you not know that you are in the neighbourhood of Gamwell-Hall?"

"So far from it," said the knight, "that I never heard the name of Gamwell-Hall before."

"Never heard of Gamwell-Hall?" exclaimed all the young women together, who could as soon have dreamed of his never having heard of the sky.

"Indeed, no," said Sir Ralph; "but I shall be very happy to get rid of my ignorance."

"And so shall I," said his squire; "for it seems that in this case knowledge will for once be a cure for hunger, wherewith I am grievously afflicted."

"And why are you so busy, my pretty damsels, weaving these garlands?" said the knight.

"Why, do you not know, sir," said one of the young women, "that to-morrow is Gamwell feast?"

The knight was again obliged, with all humility, to confess his ignorance.

"Oh! sir," said his informant, "then you will have something to see, that I can tell you; for we shall choose a Queen of the May, and we shall crown her with flowers, and place her in a chariot of flowers, and draw it with lines of flowers, and we shall hang all the trees with flowers, and we shall strew all the ground with flowers, and we shall dance with flowers, and in flowers, and on flowers, and we shall be all flowers."

"That you will," said the knight; "and the sweetest and brightest of all the flowers of the May, my pretty damsels." On which all the pretty damsels smiled at him and each other.

"And there will be all sorts of May-games, and there will be prizes for archery, and there will be the knight's ale, and the foresters' venison, and there will be Kit Scrapesqueak with his fiddle, and little Tom Whistlerap with his fife and tabor, and Sam Trumtwang with his harp, and Peter Muggledrone with his bagpipe, and how I shall dance with Will Whitethorn!" added the girl, clapping her hands as she spoke, and bounding from the ground with the pleasure of the anticipation.

A tall athletic young man approached, to whom the rustic maidens courtesied with great respect; and one of them informed Sir Ralph that it was young Master William Gamwell. The young gentleman invited and conducted the knight to the hall, where he introduced him to the old knight his father, and to the old lady his mother, and to the young lady his sister, and to a number of bold yeomen, who were laying siege to beef, brawn, and plum pie around a ponderous table, and taking copious draughts of old October. A motto was inscribed over the interior door,—

EAT, DRINK, AND BE MERRY

an injunction which Sir Ralph and his squire showed remarkable alacrity in obeying. Old Sir Guy of Gamwell gave Sir Ralph a very cordial welcome, and entertained him during supper with several of his best stories, enforced with an occasional slap on the back, and pointed with a peg in the ribs; a species of vivacious eloquence in which the old gentleman excelled, and which is supposed by many of that pleasant variety of the human spectes, known by the name of choice fellows and comical dogs, to be the genuine tangible shape of the cream of a good joke.

Chapter–VI

What! shall we have incision? shall we embrew?

***—Henry** IV*

Old Sir Guy of Gamwell, and young William Gamwell, and fair Alice Gamwell, and Sir Ralph Montfaucon and his squire, rode together the next morning to the scene of the feast. They arrived on a village green, surrounded with cottages peeping from among the trees by which the green was completely encircled. The whole circle was hung round with one continuous garland of flowers, depending in irregular festoons from the branches. In the centre of the green was a May-pole hidden in boughs and garlands; and a multitude of round-faced bumpkins and cherry-checked lasses were dancing around it, to the quadruple melody of Scrapesqueak, Whistlerap, Trumtwang, and Muggledrone: harmony we must not call it; for, though they had agreed to a partnership in point of tune, each, like a true painstaking man, seemed determined to have his time to himself: Muggledrone played allegretto, Trumtwang allegro, Whistlerap presto, and Scrapesqueak prestissimo. There was a kind of mathematical proportion in their discrepancy: while Muggledrone played the tune four times, Trumtwang played it five, Whistlerap six, and Scrapesqueak eight; for the latter completely distanced all his competitors, and indeed worked his elbow so nimbly that its outline was scarcely distinguishable through the mistiness of its rapid vibration.

While the knight was delighting his eyes and ears with these pleasant sights and sounds, all eyes were turned in one direction; and Sir Ralph, looking round, saw a fair lady in green and gold come riding through the trees, accompanied by a portly friar in grey, and several fair damsels and gallant grooms. On their nearer approach, he recognised the lady Matilda and her ghostly adviser, brother Michael. A party of foresters arrived from another direction, and then ensued cordial interchanges of greeting, and collisions of hands and lips, among the Gamwells and the new-comers,—"How does my fair coz, Mawd?" and "How does my sweet coz, Mawd?" and "How does my wild coz, Mawd?" And "Eh! jolly friar, your hand, old boy:" and "Here, honest friar:" and "To me, merry friar:" and "By your favour, mistress Alice:" and "Hey! cousin Robin:" and "Hey! cousin Will:" and "Od's life! merry Sir Guy, you grow younger every year,"—as the old knight shook them all in turn with one hand, and slapped them on the back with the other, in token of his affection. A number of young men and women advanced, some drawing, and others dancing round, a floral car; and having placed a crown of flowers on Matilda's head, they saluted her Queen of the May, and drew her to the place appointed for the rural sports.

A hogshead of ale was abroach under an oak, and a fire was blazing in an open space before the trees to roast the fat deer which the foresters brought. The sports commenced; and, after an agreeable series of bowling, coiling, pitching, hurling, racing, leaping, grinning, wrestling or friendly dislocation of joints, and cudgel-playing or amicable cracking of skulls, the trial of archery ensued. The conqueror was to be rewarded with a golden arrow from the hand of the Queen of the May, who was to be his partner in the dance till the close of the feast. This stimulated the knight's emulation: young Gamwell supplied him with a bow and arrow, and he took his station among the foresters, but had the mortification to be out-shot by them all, and to see one of them lodge the point of his arrow in the golden ring of the centre, and receive the prize from the hand of the beautiful Matilda, who smiled on him with particular grace. The jealous knight scrutinised the successful champion with great attention, and surely thought he had seen that face before. In the mean time the forester led the lady to the station. The luckless Sir Ralph drank deep draughts of love from the matchless grace of her attitudes, as, taking the bow in her left hand, and adjusting the arrow with her right, advancing her left foot, and gently curving her beautiful figure with a slight motion of her head that waved her black feathers and her ringleted hair, she drew the arrow to its head, and loosed it from her open fingers. The arrow struck within the ring of gold, so close to that of the victorious forester that the points were in contact, and the feathers were intermingled. Great acclamations succeeded, and the forester led Matilda to the dance. Sir Ralph gazed on her fascinating motions till the torments of baffled love and jealous rage became unendurable; and approaching young Gamwell, he asked him if he knew the name of that forester who was leading the dance with the Queen of the May?

"Robin, I believe," said young Gamwell carelessly; "I think they call him Robin."

"Is that all you know of him?" said Sir Ralph.

"What more should I know of him?" said young Gamwell.

"Then I can tell you," said Sir Ralph, "he is the outlawed Earl of Huntingdon, on whose head is set so large a price."

"Ay, is he?" said young Gamwell, in the same careless manner.

"He were a prize worth the taking," said Sir Ralph.

"No doubt," said young Gamwell.

"How think you?" said Sir Ralph: "are the foresters his adherents?"

"I cannot say," said young Gamwell.

"Is your peasantry loyal and well-disposed?" said Sir Ralph.

"Passing loyal," said young Gamwell.

"If I should call on them in the king's name," said Sir Ralph, "think you they would aid and assist?"

"Most likely they would," said young Gamwell, "one side or the other."

"Ay, but which side?" said the knight.

"That remains to be tried," said young Gamwell.

"I have King Henry's commission," said the knight, "to apprehend this earl that was. How would you advise me to act, being, as you see, without attendant force?"

"I would advise you," said young Gamwell, "to take yourself off without delay, unless you would relish the taste of a volley of arrows, a shower of stones, and a hailstorm of cudgel-blows, which would not be turned aside by a God save King Henry."

Sir Ralph's squire no sooner heard this, and saw by the looks of the speaker that he was not likely to prove a false prophet, than he clapped spurs to his horse and galloped off with might and main. This gave the knight a good excuse to pursue him, which he did with great celerity, calling, "Stop, you rascal." When the squire fancied himself safe out of the reach of pursuit, he checked his speed, and allowed the knight to come up with him. They rode on several miles in silence, till they discovered the towers and spires of Nottingham, where the knight introduced himself to the sheriff, and demanded an armed force to assist in the apprehension of the outlawed Earl of Huntingdon. The sheriff, who was willing to have his share of the prize, determined to accompany the knight in person, and regaled him and his man with good store of the best; after which, they, with a stout retinue of fifty men, took the way to Gamwell feast.

"God's my life," said the sheriff, as they rode along, "I had as lief you would tell me of a service of plate. I much doubt if this outlawed earl, this forester Robin, be not the man they call Robin Hood, who has quartered himself in Sherwood Forest, and whom in endeavouring to apprehend I have fallen divers times into disasters. He has gotten together a band of disinherited prodigals, outlawed debtors, excommunicated heretics, elder sons that have spent all they had, and younger sons that never had any thing to spend; and with these he kills the king's deer, and plunders wealthy travellers of five-sixths of their money; but if they be abbots or bishops, them he despoils utterly."

The sheriff then proceeded to relate to his companion the adventure of the abbot of Doubleflask (which some grave historians have related of the abbot of Saint Mary's, and others of the bishop of Hereford): how the abbot, returning to his abbey in company with his high selerer, who carried in his portmanteau the rents of the abbey-lands, and with a numerous train of attendants, came upon four seeming peasants, who were roasting the king's venison by the king's highway: how, in just indignation at this flagrant infringement of the forest laws, he asked them what they meant, and they answered that they meant to dine: how he ordered them to be seized and bound, and led captive to Nottingham, that they might know wild-flesh to have been destined by Providence for licensed and privileged appetites, and not for the base hunger of unqualified knaves: how they prayed for mercy, and how the abbot swore by Saint Charity that he would show them none: how one of them thereupon drew a bugle horn from under his smock-frock and blew three blasts, on which the abbot and his train were instantly surrounded by sixty bowmen in green: how they tied him to a tree, and made him say mass for their sins: how they unbound him, and sate him down with them to dinner, and gave him venison and wild-fowl and wine, and made him pay for his fare all the money in his high selerer's portmanteau, and enforced him to sleep all night under a tree in his cloak, and to leave the cloak behind him in the morning: how the abbot, light in pocket and heavy in heart, raised the country upon Robin Hood, for so he had heard the chief forester called by his men, and hunted him into an old woman's cottage: how Robin changed dresses with the old woman, and how the abbot rode in great triumph to Nottingham, having in custody an old woman in a green doublet and breeches: how the old woman discovered herself: how the merrymen of Nottingham laughed at the abbot: how the abbot railed at the old woman, and how the old woman out-railed the abbot, telling him that Robin had given her food and fire through the winter, which no abbot would ever do, but would rather take it from her for what he called the good of the church, by which he meant his own laziness and gluttony; and that she knew a true man from a false thief, and a free forester from a greedy abbot.

"Thus you see," added the sheriff, "how this villain perverts the deluded people by making them believe that those who tithe and toll upon them for their spiritual and temporal benefit are not their best friends and fatherly guardians; for he holds that in giving to boors and old women what he takes from priests and peers, he does but restore to the former what the latter had taken from them; and this the impudent varlet calls distributive justice. Judge now if any loyal subject can be safe in such neighbourhood."

While the sheriff was thus enlightening his companion concerning the offenders, and whetting his own indignation against them, the sun was fast sinking to the west. They rode on till they came in view of a bridge, which they saw a party approaching from the opposite side, and the knight presently discovered that the party consisted of the lady Matilda and friar Michael, young Gamwell, cousin Robin, and about half-a-dozen foresters. The knight pointed out the earl to the sheriff, who exclaimed, "Here, then, we have him an easy prey;" and they rode on manfully towards the bridge, on which the other party made halt.

"Who be these," said the friar, "that come riding so fast this way? Now, as God shall judge me, it is that false knight Sir Ralph Montfaucon, and the sheriff of Nottingham, with a posse of men. We must make good our post, and let them dislodge us if they may."

The two parties were now near enough to parley; and the sheriff and the knight, advancing in the front of the cavalcade, called on the lady, the friar, young Gamwell, and the foresters, to deliver up that false-traitor, Robert, formerly Earl of Huntingdon. Robert himself made answer by letting fly an arrow that struck the ground between the fore feet of the sheriff's horse. The horse reared up from the whizzing, and lodged the sheriff in the dust; and, at the same time, the fair Matilda favoured the knight with an arrow in his right arm, that compelled him to withdraw from the affray. His men lifted the sheriff carefully up, and replaced him on his horse, whom he immediately with great rage and zeal urged on to the assault with his fifty men at his heels, some of whom were intercepted in their advance by the arrows of the foresters and Matilda; while the friar, with an eight-foot staff, dislodged the sheriff a second time, and laid on him with all the vigour of the church militant on earth, in spite of his ejaculations of "Hey, friar Michael! What means this, honest friar? Hold, ghostly friar! Hold, holy friar!"—till Matilda interposed, and delivered the battered sheriff to the care of the foresters. The friar continued flourishing his staff among the sheriff's men, knocking down one, breaking the ribs of another, dislocating the shoulder of a third, flattening the nose of a fourth, cracking the skull of a fifth, and pitching a sixth into the river, till the few, who were lucky enough to escape with whole bones, clapped spurs to their horses and fled for their lives, under a farewell volley of arrows.

Sir Ralph's squire, meanwhile, was glad of the excuse of attending his master's wound to absent himself from the battle; and put the poor knight to a great deal of unnecessary pain by making as long a business as possible of extracting the arrow, which he had not accomplished when Matilda, approaching, extracted it with great facility, and bound up the wound with her scarf, saying, "I reclaim my arrow, sir knight, which struck where I aimed it, to admonish you to desist from your enterprise. I could as easily have lodged it in your heart."

"It did not need," said the knight, with rueful gallantry; "you have lodged one there already."

"If you mean to say that you love me," said Matilda, "it is more than I ever shall you: but if you will show your love by no further interfering with mine, you will at least merit my gratitude."

The knight made a wry face under the double pain of heart and body caused at the same moment by the material or martial, and the metaphorical or erotic arrow, of which the latter was thus barbed by a declaration more candid than flattering; but he did not choose to put in any such claim to the lady's gratitude as would bar all hopes of her love: he therefore remained silent; and the lady and her escort, leaving him and the sheriff to the care of the squire, rode on till they came in sight of Arlingford Castle, when they parted in several directions. The friar rode off alone; and after the foresters had lost sight of him they heard his voice through the twilight, singing,—

A staff, a staff, of a young oak graff,
That is both stoure and stiff,
To shrive a proud sheriffe.
And thou, fine fellowe, who hast tasted so

Of the forester's greenwood game,
Wilt be in no haste thy time to waste
In seeking more taste of the same:
Or this can I read thee, and riddle thee well,
Thou hadst better by far be the devil in hell,
Than the sheriff of Nottinghame.

❖❖❖

Chapter–VII

Now, master sheriff, what's your will with me?

–*Henry IV*

Matilda had carried her point with the baron of ranging at liberty whithersoever she would, under her positive promise to return home; she was a sort of prisoner on parole: she had obtained this indulgence by means of an obsolete habit of always telling the truth and keeping her word, which our enlightened age has discarded with other barbarisms, but which had the effect of giving her father so much confidence in her, that he could not help considering her word a better security than locks and bars.

The baron had been one of the last to hear of the rumours of the new outlaws of Sherwood, as Matilda had taken all possible precautions to keep those rumours from his knowledge, fearing that they might cause the interruption of her greenwood liberty; and it was only during her absence at Gamwell feast, that the butler, being thrown off his guard by liquor, forgot her injunctions, and regaled the baron with a long story of the right merry adventure of Robin Hood and the abbot of Doubleflask.

The baron was one morning, as usual, cutting his way valorously through a rampart of cold provision, when his ears were suddenly assailed by a tremendous alarum, and sallying forth, and looking from his castle wall, he perceived a large party of armed men on the other side of the moat, who were calling on the warder in the king's name to lower the drawbridge and raise the portcullis, which had both been secured by Matilda's order. The baron walked along the battlement till he came opposite to these unexpected visitors, who, as soon as they saw him, called out, "Lower the drawbridge, in the king's name."

"For what, in the devil's name?" said the baron.

"The sheriff of Nottingham," said one, "lies in bed grievously bruised, and many of his men are wounded, and several of them slain; and Sir Ralph Montfaucon, knight, is sore wounded in the arm; and we are charged to apprehend William Gamwell the younger, of Gamwell Hall, and father Michael of Rubygill Abbey, and Matilda Fitzwater of Arlingford Castle, as agents and accomplices in the said breach of the king's peace."

"Breach of the king's fiddlestick!" answered the baron. "What do you mean by coming here with your cock and bull, stories of my daughter grievously bruising the sheriff of Nottingham? You are a set of vagabond rascals in disguise; and I hear, by the bye, there is a gang of thieves that has just set up business in Sherwood Forest: a pretty presence, indeed, to get into my castle with force and arms, and make a famine in my buttery, and a drought in my cellar, and a void in my strong box, and a vacuum in my silver scullery."

"Lord Fitzwater," cried one, "take heed how you resist lawful authority: we will prove ourselves—"

"You will prove yourselves arrant knaves, I doubt not," answered the baron; "but, villains, you shall be more grievously bruised by me than ever was the sheriff by my daughter (a pretty tale truly!), if you do not forthwith avoid my territory."

By this time the baron's men had flocked to the battlements, with long-bows and cross-bows, slings and stones, and Matilda with her bow and quiver at their head. The assailants, finding the castle so well defended, deemed it expedient to withdraw till they could return in greater force, and rode off to Rubygill

Abbey, where they made known their errand to the father abbot, who, having satisfied himself of their legitimacy, and conned over the allegations, said that doubtless brother Michael had heinously offended; but it was not for the civil law to take cognizance of the misdoings of a holy friar; that he would summon a chapter of monks, and pass on the offender a sentence proportionate to his offence. The ministers of civil justice said that would not do. The abbot said it would do and should; and bade them not provoke the meekness of his catholic charity to lay them under the curse of Rome. This threat had its effect, and the party rode off to Gamwell-Hall, where they found the Gamwells and their men just sitting down to dinner, which they saved them the trouble of eating by consuming it in the king's name themselves, having first seized and bound young Gamwell; all which they accomplished by dint of superior numbers, in despite of a most vigorous stand made by the Gamwellites in defence of their young master and their provisions.

The baron, meanwhile, after the ministers of justice had departed, interrogated Matilda concerning the alleged fact of the grievous bruising of the sheriff of Nottingham. Matilda told him the whole history of Gamwell feast, and of their battle on the bridge, which had its origin in a design of the sheriff of Nottingham to take one of the foresters into custody.

"Ay! ay!" said the baron, "and I guess who that forester was; but truly this friar is a desperate fellow. I did not think there could have been so much valour under a grey frock. And so you wounded the knight in the arm. You are a wild girl, Mawd,—a chip of the old block, Mawd. A wild girl, and a wild friar, and three or four foresters, wild lads all, to keep a bridge against a tame knight, and a tame sheriff, and fifty tame varlets; by this light, the like was never heard! But do you know, Mawd, you must not go about so any more, sweet Mawd: you must stay at home, you must ensconce; for there is your tame sheriff on the one hand, that will take you perforce; and there is your wild forester on the other hand, that will take you without any force at all, Mawd: your wild forester, Robin, cousin Robin, Robin Hood of Sherwood Forest, that beats and binds bishops, spreads nets for archbishops, and hunts a fat abbot as if he were a buck: excellent game, no doubt, but you must hunt no more in such company. I see it now: truly I might have guessed before that the bold outlaw Robin, the most courteous Robin, the new thief of Sherwood Forest, was your lover, the earl that has been: I might have guessed it before, and what led you so much to the woods; but you hunt no more in such company. No more May games and Gamwell feasts. My lands and castle would be the forfeit of a few more such pranks; and I think they are as well in my hands as the king's, quite as well."

"You know, father," said Matilda, "the condition of keeping me at home: I get out if I can, and not on parole."

"Ay! ay!" said the baron, "if you can; very true: watch and ward, Mawd, watch and ward is my word: if you can, is yours. The mark is set, and so start fair."

The baron would have gone on in this way for an hour; but the friar made his appearance with a long oak staff in his hand, singing,—

Drink and sing, and eat and laugh,
And so go forth to battle:
For the top of a skull and the end of a staff
Do make a ghostly rattle.

"Ho! ho! friar!" said the baron—"singing friar, laughing friar, roaring friar, fighting friar, hacking friar, thwacking friar; cracking, cracking, cracking friar; joke-cracking, bottle-cracking, skull-cracking friar!"

"And ho! ho!" said the friar,—"bold baron, old baron, sturdy baron, wordy baron, long baron, strong baron, mighty baron, flighty baron, mazed baron, crazed baron, hacked baron, thwacked baron; cracked, cracked, cracked baron; bone-cracked, sconce-cracked, brain-cracked baron!"

"What do you mean," said the baron, "bully friar, by calling me hacked and thwacked?"

"Were you not in the wars?" said the friar, "where he who escapes untracked does more credit to his heels than his arms. I pay tribute to your valour in calling you hacked and thwacked."

"I never was thwacked in my life," said the baron; "I stood my ground manfully, and covered my body with my sword. If I had had the luck to meet with a fighting friar indeed, I might have been thwacked, and soundly too; but I hold myself a match for any two laymen; it takes nine fighting laymen to make a fighting friar."

"Whence come you now, holy father?" asked Matilda.

"From Rubygill Abbey," said the friar, "whither I never return:

For I must seek some hermit cell,
Where I alone my beads may tell,
And on the wight who that way fares
evy a toll for my ghostly pray'rs,
Levy a toll, levy a toll,
Levy a toll for my ghostly pray'rs."

"What is the matter then, father?" said Matilda.

"This is the matter," said the friar: "my holy brethren have held a chapter on me, and sentenced me to seven years' privation of wine. I therefore deemed it fitting to take my departure, which they would fain have prohibited. I was enforced to clear the way with my staff. I have grievously beaten my dearly beloved brethren: I grieve thereat; but they enforced me thereto. I have beaten them much; I mowed them down to the right and to the left, and left them like an ill-reaped field of wheat, ear and straw pointing all ways, scattered in singleness and jumbled in masses; and so bade them farewell, saying, Peace be with you. But I must not tarry, lest danger be in my rear: therefore, farewell, sweet Matilda; and farewell, noble baron; and farewell, sweet Matilda again, the alpha and omega of father Michael, the first and the last."

"Farewell, father," said the baron, a little softened; "and God send you be never assailed by more than fifty men at a time."

"Amen," said the friar, "to that good wish."

"And we shall meet again, father, I trust," said Matilda.

"When the storm is blown over," said the baron.

"Doubt it not," said the friar, "though flooded Trent were between us, and fifty devils guarded the bridge."

He kissed Matilda's forehead, and walked away without a song.

❖❖❖

Chapter–VIII

Let gallows gape for dog: let man go free.

–Henry V

A page had been brought up in Gamwell-Hall, who, while he was little, had been called Little John, and continued to be so called after he had grown to be a foot taller than any other man in the house. He was full seven feet high. His latitude was worthy of his longitude, and his strength was worthy of both; and though an honest man by profession, he had practiced archery on the king's deer for the benefit of his master's household, and for the improvement of his own eye and hand, till his aim had become infallible within the range of two miles. He had fought manfully in defence of his young master, took his captivity exceedingly to heart, and fell into bitter grief and boundless rage when he heard that he had been tried in Nottingham and sentenced to die. Alice Gamwell, at Little John's request, wrote three letters of one tenour; and Little John, having attached them to three blunt arrows, saddled the fleetest steed in old Sir Guy of Gamwell's stables, mounted, and rode first to Arlingford Castle, where he shot one of the three arrows over the battlements; then to Rubygill Abbey, where he shot the second into the abbey-garden; then back past Gamwell-Hall to the borders of Sherwood Forest, where he shot the third into the wood. Now the first of these arrows lighted in the nape of the neck of Lord Fitzwater, and lodged itself firmly between his skin and his collar; the second rebounded with the hollow vibration of a drumstick from the shaven sconce of the abbot of Rubygill; and the third pitched perpendicularly into the centre of a venison pasty in which Robin Hood was making incision.

Matilda ran up to her father in the court of Arlingford Castle, seized the arrow, drew off the letter, and concealed it in her bosom before the baron had time to look round, which he did with many expressions of rage against the impudent villain who had shot a blunt arrow into the nape of his neck.

"But you know, father," said Matilda, "a sharp arrow in the same place would have killed you; therefore the sending a blunt one was very considerate."

"Considerate, with a vengeance!" said the baron. "Where was the consideration of sending it at all? This is some of your forester's pranks. He has missed you in the forest, since I have kept watch and ward over you, and by way of a love-token and a remembrance to you takes a random shot at me."

The abbot of Rubygill picked up the missile-missive or messenger arrow, which had rebounded from his shaven crown, with a very unghostly malediction on the sender, which he suddenly checked with a pious and consolatory reflection on the goodness of Providence in having blessed him with such a thickness of skull, to which he was now indebted for temporal preservation, as he had before been for spiritual promotion. He opened the letter, which was addressed to father Michael; and found it to contain an intimation that William Gamwell was to be hanged on Monday at Nottingham.

"And I wish," said the abbot, "father Michael were to be hanged with him: an ungrateful monster, after I had rescued him from the fangs of civil justice, to reward my lenity by not leaving a bone unbruised among the holy brotherhood of Rubygill."

Robin Hood extracted from his venison pasty a similar intimation of the evil destiny of his cousin, whom he determined, if possible, to rescue from the jaws of Cerberus.

The sheriff of Nottingham, though still sore with his bruises, was so intent on revenge, that he raised himself from his bed to attend the execution of William Gamwell. He rode to the august structure of retributive Themis, as the French call a gallows, in all the pride and pomp of shrievalty, and with a splendid retinue of well-equipped knaves and varlets, as our ancestors called honest serving-men.

Young Gamwell was brought forth with his arms pinioned behind him; his sister Alice and his father, Sir Guy, attending him in disconsolate mood. He had rejected the confessor provided by the sheriff, and had insisted on the privilege of choosing his own, whom Little John had promised to bring. Little John, however, had not made his appearance when the fatal procession began its march; but when they reached the place of execution, Little John appeared, accompanied by a ghostly friar.

"Sheriff," said young Gamwell, "let me not die with my hands pinioned: give me a sword, and set any odds of your men against me, and let me die the death of a man, like the descendant of a noble house, which has never yet been stained with ignominy."

"No, no," said the sheriff; "I have had enough of setting odds against you. I have sworn you shall be hanged, and hanged you shall be."

"Then God have mercy on me," said young Gamwell; "and now, holy friar, shrive my sinful soul."

The friar approached.

"Let me see this friar," said the sheriff: "if he be the friar of the bridge, I had as lief have the devil in Nottingham; but he shall find me too much for him here."

"The friar of the bridge," said Little John, "as you very well know, sheriff, was father Michael of Rubygill Abbey, and you may easily see that this is not the man."

"I see it," said the sheriff; "and God be thanked for his absence."

Young Gamwell stood at the foot of the ladder. The friar approached him, opened his book, groaned, turned up the whites of his eyes, tossed up his arms in the air, and said "Dominus vobiscum." He then crossed both his hands on his breast under the folds of his holy robes, and stood a few moments as if in inward prayer. A deep silence among the attendant crowd accompanied this action of the friar; interrupted only by the hollow tone of the death-bell, at long and dreary intervals. Suddenly the friar threw off his holy robes, and appeared a forester clothed in green, with a sword in his right hand and a horn in his left. With the sword he cut the bonds of William Gamwell, who instantly snatched a sword from one of the sheriff's men; and with the horn he blew a loud blast, which was answered at once by four bugles from the quarters of the four winds, and from each quarter came five-and-twenty bowmen running all on a row.

"Treason! treason!" cried the sheriff. Old Sir Guy sprang to his son's side, and so did Little John; and the four setting back to back, kept the sheriff and his men at bay till the bowmen came within shot and let fly their arrows among the sheriff's men, who, after a brief resistance, fled in all directions. The forester, who had personated the friar, sent an arrow after the flying sheriff, calling with a strong voice, "To the sheriff's left arm, as a keepsake from Robin Hood." The arrow reached its destiny; the sheriff redoubled his speed, and, with the one arrow in his arm, did not stop to breathe till he was out of reach of another.

The foresters did not waste time in Nottingham, but were soon at a distance from its walls. Sir Guy returned with Alice to Gamwell-Hall; but thinking he should not be safe there, from the share he had had in his son's rescue, they only remained long enough to supply themselves with clothes and money, and departed, under the escort of Little John, to another seat of the Gamwells in Yorkshire. Young Gamwell, taking it for granted that his offence was past remission, determined on joining Robin Hood, and accompanied him to the forest, where it was deemed expedient that he should change his name; and he was rechristened without a priest, and with wine instead of water, by the immortal name of Scarlet.

❖❖❖

Chapter–IX

Who set my man i' the stocks? –
I set him there, Sir but his own disordersDeserved much less advancement

–Lear

The baron was inflexible in his resolution not to let Matilda leave the castle. The letter, which announced to her the approaching fate of young Gamwell, filled her with grief, and increased the irksomeness of a privation which already preyed sufficiently on her spirits, and began to undermine her health. She had no longer the consolation of the society of her old friend father Michael: the little fat friar of Rubygill was substituted as the castle confessor, not without some misgivings in his ghostly bosom; but he was more allured by the sweet savour of the good things of this world at Arlingford Castle, than deterred by his awe of the lady Matilda, which nevertheless was so excessive, from his recollection of the twang of the bow-string, that he never ventured to find her in the wrong, much less to enjoin any thing in the shape of penance, as was the occasional practice of holy confessors, with or without cause, for the sake of pious discipline, and what was in those days called social order, namely, the preservation of the privileges of the few who happened to have any, at the expense of the swinish multitude who happened to have none, except that of working and being shot at for the benefit of their betters, which is obviously not the meaning of social order in our more enlightened times: let us therefore be grateful to Providence, and sing Te Deum laudamus in chorus with the Holy Alliance.

The little friar, however, though he found the lady spotless, found the butler a great sinner: at least so it was conjectured, from the length of time he always took to confess him in the buttery.

Matilda became every day more pale and dejected: her spirit, which could have contended against any strenuous affliction, pined in the monotonous inaction to which she was condemned. While she could freely range the forest with her lover in the morning, she had been content to return to her father's castle in the evening, thus preserving underanged the balance of her duties, habits, and affections; not without a hope that the repeal of her lover's outlawry might be eventually obtained, by a judicious distribution of some of his forest spoils among the holy fathers and saints that-were-to-be,—pious proficients in the ecclesiastic art equestrian, who rode the conscience of King Henry with double-curb bridles, and kept it well in hand when it showed mettle and seemed inclined to rear and plunge. But the affair at Gamwell feast threw many additional difficulties in the way of the accomplishment of this hope; and very shortly afterwards King Henry the Second went to make up in the next world his quarrel with Thomas-a-Becket; and Richard Coeur de Lion made all England resound with preparations for the crusade, to the great delight of many zealous adventurers, who eagerly flocked under his banner in the hope of enriching themselves with Saracen spoil, which they called fighting the battles of God. Richard, who was not remarkably scrupulous in his financial operations, was not likely to overlook the lands and castle of Locksley, which he appropriated immediately to his own purposes, and sold to the highest bidder. Now, as the repeal of the outlawry would involve the restitution of the estates to the rightful owner, it was obvious that it could never be expected from that most legitimate and most Christian king, Richard the First of England, the arch-crusader and anti-jacobin by excellence,—the very type, flower, cream, pink, symbol, and mirror of all the Holy Alliances that have ever existed on earth, excepting that he seasoned his superstition and love of conquest with a certain condiment of romantic generosity and chivalrous self-devotion, with which his imitators in all other points have found it convenient to dispense. To give freely to one man what he had taken forcibly from another, was generosity of which he was very capable; but to restore what he had taken to the man from whom he had taken it, was something that wore too much of the cool physiognomy of justice to be easily reconcileable to his kingly feelings. He had, besides, not only sent all King Henry's saints about their business, or rather about their no-business—their faineantise—but he had laid them under rigorous contribution for the purposes of his holy war; and having made them refund to the piety of the successor what they had extracted from the piety of the precursor, he compelled them, in addition, to give him their blessing for nothing. Matilda, therefore, from all these circumstances, felt little hope that her lover would be any thing but an outlaw for life.

The departure of King Richard from England was succeeded by the episcopal regency of the bishops of Ely and Durham. Longchamp, bishop of Ely, proceeded to show his sense of Christian fellowship by arresting his brother bishop, and despoiling him of his share in the government; and to set forth his humility and loving-kindness in a retinue of nobles and knights who consumed in one night's entertainment some five years' revenue of their entertainer, and in a guard of fifteen hundred foreign soldiers, whom he considered indispensable to the exercise of a vigour beyond the law in maintaining wholesome discipline over the refractory English. The ignorant impatience of the swinish multitude with these fruits of good living, brought forth by one of the meek who had inherited the earth, displayed itself in a general ferment, of which Prince John took advantage to make the experiment of getting possession of his brother's crown in his absence. He began by calling at Reading a council of barons, whose aspect induced the holy bishop to disguise himself (some say as an old woman, which, in the twelfth century, perhaps might have been a disguise for a bishop), and make his escape beyond sea. Prince John followed up his advantage by obtaining possession of several strong posts, and among others of the castle of Nottingham.

While John was conducting his operations at Nottingham, he rode at times past the castle of Arlingford. He stopped on one occasion to claim Lord Fitzwater's hospitality, and made most princely havoc among his venison and brawn. Now it is a matter of record among divers great historians and learned clerks, that he was then and there grievously smitten by the charms of the lovely Matilda, and that a few days after he despatched his travelling minstrel, or laureate, Harpiton, [3](whom he retained at moderate wages, to keep a journal of his proceedings, and prove them all just and legitimate), to the castle of Arlingford, to make proposals to the lady. This Harpiton was a very useful person. He was always ready, not only to maintain the cause of his master with his pen, and to sing his eulogies to his harp, but to undertake at a moment's notice any kind of courtly employment, called dirty work by the profane, which the blessings of civil government, namely, his master's pleasure, and the interests of social order, namely, his own emolument, might require. In short,

Il eut l'emploi qui certes n'est pas mince,
Et qu'a la cour, ou tout se peint en beau,
On appelloit etre l'ami du prince;

---

[3] Harp-it-on: or, a corruption of (greek 'Erpeton), a creeping thing.

Mais qu'a la ville, et surtout en province,
Les gens grossiers ont nomme maquereau.

Prince John was of opinion that the love of a prince actual and king expectant, was in itself a sufficient honour to the daughter of a simple baron, and that the right divine or royalty would make it sufficiently holy without the rite divine of the church. He was, therefore, graciously pleased to fall into an exceeding passion, when his confidential messenger returned from his embassy in piteous plight, having been, by the baron's order, first tossed in a blanket and set in the stocks to cool, and afterwards ducked in the moat and set again in the stocks to dry. John swore to revenge horribly this flagrant outrage on royal prerogative, and to obtain possession of the lady by force of arms; and accordingly collected a body of troops, and marched upon Arlingford castle. A letter, conveyed as before on the point of a blunt arrow, announced his approach to Matilda: and lord Fitzwater had just time to assemble his retainers, collect a hasty supply of provision, raise the draw-bridge, and drop the portcullis, when the castle was surrounded by the enemy. The little fat friar, who during the confusion was asleep in the buttery, found himself, on awaking, inclosed in the besieged castle, and dolefully bewailed his evil chance.

Chapter–X

A noble girl, i' faith. Heart! I think I fight with a familiar, or the ghost of a fencer. Call you this an amorous visage? Here's blood that would have served me these seven years, in broken heads and cut fingers, and now it runs out all together

–Middleton. Roaring Girl

Prince John sat down impatiently before Arlingford castle in the hope of starving out the besieged; but finding the duration of their supplies extend itself in an equal ratio with the prolongation of his hope, he made vigorous preparations for carrying the place by storm. He constructed an immense machine on wheels, which, being advanced to the edge of the moat, would lower a temporary bridge, of which one end would rest on the bank, and the other on the battlements, and which, being well furnished with stepping boards, would enable his men to ascend the inclined plane with speed and facility. Matilda received intimation of this design by the usual friendly channel of a blunt arrow, which must either have been sent from some secret friend in the prince's camp, or from some vigorous archer beyond it: the latter will not appear improbable, when we consider that Robin Hood and Little John could shoot two English miles and an inch point-blank,

Come scrive Turpino, che non erra.

The machine was completed, and the ensuing morning fixed for the assault. Six men, relieved at intervals, kept watch over it during the night. Prince John retired to sleep, congratulating himself in the expectation that another day would place the fair culprit at his princely mercy. His anticipations mingled with the visions of his slumber, and he dreamed of wounds and drums, and sacking and firing the castle, and bearing off in his arms the beautiful prize through the midst of fire and smoke. In the height of this imaginary turmoil, he awoke, and conceived for a few moments that certain sounds which rang in his ears, were the continuation of those of his dream, in that sort of half-consciousness between sleeping and waking, when reality and phantasy meet and mingle in dim and confused resemblance. He was, however, very soon fully awake to the fact of his guards calling on him to arm, which he did in haste, and beheld the machine in flames, and a furious conflict raging around it. He hurried to the spot, and found that his camp had been suddenly assailed from one side by a party of foresters, and that the baron's people had made a sortie on the other, and that they had killed the guards, and set fire to the machine, before the rest of the camp could come to the assistance of their fellows.

The night was in itself intensely dark, and the fire-light shed around it a vivid and unnatural radiance. On one side, the crimson light quivered by its own agitation on the waveless moat, and on the bastions and buttresses of the castle, and their shadows lay in massy blackness on the illuminated walls: on the other, it shone upon the woods, streaming far within among the open trunks, or resting on the closer foliage. The circumference of darkness bounded the scene on all sides: and in the centre raged the war; shields, helmets, and bucklers gleaming and glittering as they rang and clashed against each other; plumes confusedly tossing in the crimson light, and the messy light and shade that fell on the faces of the combatants, giving additional energy to their ferocious expression.

John, drawing nearer to the scene of action, observed two young warriors fighting side by side, one of whom wore the habit of a forester, the other that of a retainer of Arlingford. He looked intently on them both: their position towards the fire favoured the scrutiny; and the hawk's eye of love very speedily discovered that the latter was the fair Matilda. The forester he did not know: but he had sufficient tact to discern that his success would be very much facilitated by separating her from this companion, above all others. He therefore formed a party of men into a wedge, only taking especial care not to be the point of it himself, and drove it between them with so much precision, that they were in a moment far asunder.

"Lady Matilda," said John, "yield yourself my prisoner."

"If you would wear me, prince," said Matilda, "you must win me:" and without giving him time to deliberate on the courtesy of fighting with the lady of his love, she raised her sword in the air, and lowered it on his head with an impetus that would have gone nigh to fathom even that extraordinary depth of brain which always by divine grace furnishes the interior of a head-royal, if he had not very dexterously parried the blow. Prince John wished to disarm and take captive, not in any way to wound or injure, least of all to kill, his fair opponent. Matilda was only intent to get rid of her antagonist at any rate: the edge of her weapon painted his complexion with streaks of very unloverlike crimson, and she would probably have marred John's hand for ever signing Magna Charta, but that he was backed by the advantage of numbers, and that her sword broke short on the boss of his buckler. John was following up his advantage to make a captive of the lady, when he was suddenly felled to the earth by an unseen antagonist. Some of his men picked him carefully up, and conveyed him to his tent, stunned and stupified.

When he recovered, he found Harpiton diligently assisting in his recovery, more in the fear of losing his place than in that of losing his master: the prince's first inquiry was for the prisoner he had been on the point of taking at the moment when his habeas corpus was so unseasonably suspended. He was told that his people had been on the point of securing the said prisoner, when the devil suddenly appeared among them in the likeness of a tall friar, having his grey frock cinctured with a sword-belt, and his crown, which whether it were shaven or no they could not see, surmounted with a helmet, and flourishing an eight-foot staff, with which he laid about him to the right and to the left, knocking down the prince and his men as if they had been so many nine-pins: in fine, he had rescued the prisoner, and made a clear passage through friend and foe, and in conjunction with a chosen party of archers, had covered the retreat of the baron's men and the foresters, who had all gone off in a body towards Sherwood forest.

Harpiton suggested that it would be desirable to sack the castle, and volunteered to lead the van on the occasion, as the defenders were withdrawn, and the exploit seemed to promise much profit and little danger: John considered that the castle would in itself be a great acquisition to him, as a stronghold in furtherance of his design on his brother's throne; and was determining to take possession with the first light of morning, when he had the mortification to see the castle burst into flames in several places at once. A piteous cry was heard from within, and while the prince was proclaiming a reward to any one who would enter into the burning pile, and elucidate the mystery of the doleful voice, forth waddled the little fat friar in an agony of fear, out of the fire into the frying-pan; for he was instantly taken into custody and carried before Prince John, wringing his hands and tearing his hair.

"Are you the friar," said Prince John, in a terrible voice, "that laid me prostrate in battle, mowed down my men like grass, rescued my captive, and covered the retreat of my enemies? And, not content with this, have you now set fire to the castle in which I intended to take up my royal quarters?"

The little friar quaked like a jelly: he fell on his knees, and attempted to speak; but in his eagerness to vindicate himself from this accumulation of alarming charges, he knew not where to begin; his ideas rolled round upon each other like the radii of a wheel; the words he desired to utter, instead of issuing, as it were, in a right line from his lips, seemed to conglobate themselves into a sphere turning on its own axis in his throat: after several ineffectual efforts, his utterance totally failed him, and he remained gasping, with his mouth open, his lips quivering, his hands clasped together, and the whites of his eyes turned up towards the prince with an expression most ruefully imploring.

"Are you that friar?" repeated the prince.

Several of the by-standers declared that he was not that friar. The little friar, encouraged by this patronage, found his voice, and pleaded for mercy. The prince questioned him closely concerning the burning of the castle. The little friar declared, that he had been in too great fear during the siege to know much of what was going forward, except that he had been conscious during the last few days of a lamentable deficiency of provisions, and had been present that very morning at the broaching of the last butt of sack. Harpiton groaned in sympathy. The little friar added, that he knew nothing of what had passed since till he heard the flames roaring at his elbow.

"Take him away, Harpiton," said the prince, "fill him with sack, and turn him out."

"Never mind the sack," said the little friar, "turn me out at once."

"A sad chance," said Harpiton, "to be turned out without sack."

But what Harpiton thought a sad chance the little friar thought a merry one, and went bounding like a fat buck towards the abbey of Rubygill.

An arrow, with a letter attached to it, was shot into the camp, and carried to the prince. The contents were these:—

"Prince John,—I do not consider myself to have resisted lawful authority in defending my castle against you, seeing that you are at present in a state of active rebellion against your liege sovereign Richard: and if my provisions had not failed me, I would have maintained it till doomsday. As it is, I have so well disposed my combustibles that it shall not serve you as a strong hold in your rebellion. If you hunt in the chases of Nottinghamshire, you may catch other game than my daughter. Both she and I are content to be houseless for a time, in the reflection that we have deserved your enmity, and the friendship of Coeur-de-Lion.

"FITZWATER."

Chapter–XI

Tuck, the merry friar, who many a sermon made In praise of Robin Hood, his outlaws, and their trade.

–Drayton

The baron, with some of his retainers and all the foresters, halted at daybreak in Sherwood forest. The foresters quickly erected tents, and prepared an abundant breakfast of venison and ale.

"Now, Lord Fitzwater," said the chief forester, "recognise your son-in-law that was to have been, in the outlaw Robin Hood."

"Ay, ay," said the baron, "I have recognised you long ago."

"And recognise your young friend Gamwell," said the second, "in the outlaw Scarlet."

"And Little John, the page," said the third, "in Little John the outlaw."

"And Father Michael, of Rubygill Abbey," said the friar, "in Friar Tuck, of Sherwood forest. Truly, I have a chapel here hard by, in the shape of a hollow tree, where I put up my prayers for travellers, and Little John holds the plate at the door, for good praying deserves good paying."

"I am in fine company," said the baron.

"In the very best of company," said the friar, "in the high court of Nature, and in the midst of her own nobility. Is it not so? This goodly grove is our palace: the oak and the beech are its colonnade and its canopy: the sun and the moon and the stars are its everlasting lamps: the grass, and the daisy, and the primrose, and the violet, are its many-coloured floor of green, white, yellow, and blue; the may-flower, and the woodbine, and the eglantine, and the ivy, are its decorations, its curtains, and its tapestry: the lark, and the thrush, and the linnet, and the nightingale, are its unhired minstrels and musicians. Robin Hood is king of the forest both by dignity of birth and by virtue of his standing army: to say nothing of the free choice of his people, which he has indeed, but I pass it by as an illegitimate basis of power. He holds his dominion over the forest, and its horned multitude of citizen-deer, and its swinish multitude or peasantry of wild boars, by right of conquest and force of arms. He levies contributions among them by the free consent of his archers, their virtual representatives. If they should find a voice to complain that we are 'tyrants and usurpers to kill and cook them up in their assigned and native dwelling-place,' we should most convincingly admonish them, with point of arrow, that they have nothing to do with our laws but to obey them. Is it not written that the fat ribs of the herd shall be fed upon by the mighty in the land? And have not they withal my blessing? my orthodox, canonical, and archiepiscopal blessing? Do I not give thanks for them when they are well roasted and smoking under my nose? What title had William of Normandy to England, that Robin of Locksley has not to merry Sherwood? William fought for his claim. So does Robin. With whom, both? With any that would or will dispute it. William raised contributions. So does Robin. From whom, both? From all that they could or can make pay them. Why did any pay them to William? Why do any pay them to Robin? For the same reason to both: because they could not or cannot help it. They differ indeed, in this, that William took from the poor and gave to the rich, and Robin takes from the rich and gives to the poor: and therein is Robin illegitimate; though in all else he is true prince. Scarlet and John, are they not peers of the forest? lords temporal of Sherwood? And am not I lord spiritual? Am I not archbishop? Am I not pope? Do I not consecrate their banner and absolve their sins? Are not they state, and am not I church? Are not they state monarchical, and am not I church militant? Do I not excommunicate our enemies from venison and brawn, and by 'r Lady, when need calls, beat them down under my feet? The state levies tax, and the church levies tithe. Even so do we. Mass, we take all at once. What then? It is tax by redemption and tithe by commutation. Your William and Richard can cut and come again, but our Robin deals with slippery subjects that come not twice to his exchequer. What need we then to constitute a court, except a fool and a laureate? For the fool, his only use is to make false knaves merry by art, and we are true men and are merry by nature. For the laureate, his only office is to find virtues in those who have none, and to drink sack for his pains. We have quite virtue enough to need him not, and can drink our sack for ourselves." "Well preached, friar," said Robin Hood: "yet there is one thing wanting to constitute a court, and that is a queen. And now, lovely Matilda, look round upon these sylvan shades where we have so often roused the stag from his ferny covert. The rising sun smiles upon us through the stems of that beechen knoll. Shall I take your hand, Matilda, in the presence of this my court? Shall I crown you with our wild-wood coronal, and hail you queen of the forest? Will you be the queen Matilda of your own true king Robin?"

Matilda smiled assent.

"Not Matilda," said the friar: "the rules of our holy alliance require new birth. We have excepted in favour of Little John, because he is great John, and his name is a misnomer. I sprinkle, not thy forehead with water, but thy lips with wine, and baptize thee MARIAN."

"Here is a pretty conspiracy," exclaimed the baron. "Why, you villanous friar, think you to nickname and marry my daughter before my face with impunity?"

"Even so, bold baron," said the friar; "we are strongest here. Say you, might overcomes right? I say no. There is no right but might: and to say that might overcomes right is to say that right overcomes itself: an absurdity most palpable. Your right was the stronger in Arlingford, and ours is the stronger in Sherwood. Your right was right as long as you could maintain it; so is ours. So is King Richard's, with all deference be it spoken; and so is King Saladin's; and their two mights are now committed in bloody fray, and that which overcomes will be right, just as long as it lasts, and as far as it reaches. And now if any of you know any just impediment—"

"Fire and fury," said the baron.

"Fire and fury," said the friar, "are modes of that might which constitutes right, and are just impediments to any thing against which they can be brought to bear. They are our good allies upon occasion, and would declare for us now if you should put them to the test."

"Father," said Matilda, "you know the terms of our compact: from the moment you restrained my liberty, you renounced your claim to all but compulsory obedience. The friar argues well. Right ends with might. Thick walls, dreary galleries, and tapestried chambers, were indifferent to me while I could leave them at pleasure, but have ever been hateful to me since they held me by force. May I never again have roof but the blue sky, nor canopy but the green leaves, nor barrier but the forest-bounds; with the foresters to my train, Little John to my page, Friar Tuck to my ghostly adviser, and Robin Hood to my liege lord. I am no longer lady Matilda Fitzwater, of Arlingford Castle, but plain Maid Marian, of Sherwood Forest."

"Long live Maid Marian!" re-echoed the foresters.

"Oh false girl!" said the baron, "do you renounce your name and parentage?"

"Not my parentage," said Marian, "but my name indeed: do not all maids renounce it at the altar?"

"The altar!" said the baron: "grant me patience! what do you mean by the altar?"

"Pile green turf," said the friar, "wreathe it with flowers, and crown it with fruit, and we will show the noble baron what we mean by the altar."

The foresters did as the friar directed.

"Now, Little John," said the friar, "on with the cloak of the abbot of Doubleflask. I appoint thee my clerk: thou art here duly elected in full mote."

"I wish you were all in full moat together," said the baron, "and smooth wall on both sides."

"Punnest thou?" said the friar. "A heinous anti-christian offence. Why anti-christian? Because anti-catholic? Why anti-catholic? Because anti-roman. Why anti-roman? Because Carthaginian. Is not pun from Punic? punica fides: the very quint-essential quiddity of bad faith: double-visaged: double-tongued. He that will make a pun will— I say no more. Fie on it. Stand forth, clerk. Who is the bride's father?"

"There is no bride's father," said the baron. "I am the father of Matilda Fitzwater."

"There is none such," said the friar. "This is the fair Maid Marian. Will you make a virtue of necessity, or will you give laws to the flowing tide? Will you give her, or shall Robin take her? Will you be her true natural father, or shall I commute paternity? Stand forth, Scarlet."

"Stand back, sirrah Scarlet," said the baron. "My daughter shall have no father but me. Needs must when the devil drives."

"No matter who drives," said the friar, "so that, like a well-disposed subject, you yield cheerful obedience to those who can enforce it."

"Mawd, sweet Mawd," said the baron, "will you then forsake your poor old father in his distress, with his castle in ashes, and his enemy in power?"

"Not so, father," said Marian; "I will always be your true daughter: I will always love, and serve, and watch, and defend you: but neither will I forsake my plighted love, and my own liege lord, who was your choice before he was mine, for you made him my associate in infancy; and that he continued to be mine when he ceased to be yours, does not in any way show remissness in my duties or falling off in my affections. And though I here plight my troth at the altar to Robin, in the presence of this holy priest and pious clerk, yet.... Father, when Richard returns from Palestine, he will restore you to your barony, and perhaps, for your sake, your daughter's husband to the earldom of Huntingdon: should that never be, should it be the will of fate that we must live and die in the greenwood, I will live and die MAID MARIAN." [4]

"A pretty resolution," said the baron, "if Robin will let you keep it."

"I have sworn it," said Robin. "Should I expose her tenderness to the perils of maternity, when life and death may hang on shifting at a moment's notice from Sherwood to Barnsdale, and from Barnsdale to the sea-shore? And why should I banquet when my merry men starve? Chastity is our forest law, and even the friar has kept it since he has been here."

"Truly so," said the friar: "for temptation dwells with ease and luxury: but the hunter is Hippolytus, and the huntress is Dian. And now, dearly beloved—"

---

[4] Erpeton), a creeping thing.

The friar went through the ceremony with great unction, and Little John was most clerical in the intonation of his responses. After which, the friar sang, and Little John fiddled, and the foresters danced, Robin with Marian, and Scarlet with the baron; and the venison smoked, and the ale frothed, and the wine sparkled, and the sun went down on their unwearied festivity: which they wound up with the following song, the friar leading and the foresters joining chorus:

Oh! bold Robin Hood is a forester good,
As ever drew bow in the merry greenwood:
At his bugle's shrill singing the echoes are ringing,
The wild deer are springing for many a rood:
Its summons we follow, through brake, over hollow,
The thrice-blown shrill summons of bold Robin Hood.

And what eye hath e'er seen such a sweet Maiden Queen,
As Marian, the pride of the forester's green?
A sweet garden-flower, she blooms in the bower,
Where alone to this hour the wild rose has been:
We hail her in duty the queen of all beauty:
We will live, we will die, by our sweet Maiden queen.

And here's a grey friar, good as heart can desire,
To absolve all our sins as the case may require:
Who with courage so stout, lays his oak-plant about,
And puts to the rout all the foes of his choir:
For we are his choristers, we merry foresters,
Chorussing thus with our militant friar

And Scarlet cloth bring his good yew-bough and string,
Prime minister is he of Robin our king:
No mark is too narrow for little John's arrow,
That hits a cock sparrow a mile on the wing;
Robin and Marion, Scarlet, and Little John,
Long with their glory old Sherwood shall ring.
Each a good liver, for well-feathered quiver

Doth furnish brawn, venison, and fowl of the river:
But the best game we dish up, it is a fat bishop:
When his angels we fish up, he proves a free giver:
For a prelate so lowly has angels more holy,
And should this world's false angels to sinners deliver.

Robin and Marion, Scarlet and Little John,
Drink to them one by one, drink as ye sing:
Robin and Marion, Scarlet and Little John,
Echo to echo through Sherwood shall fling:
Robin and Marion, Scarlet and Little John,
Long with their glory old Sherwood shall ring.

Chapter–XII

A single volume paramount: a code
A master spirit: a determined road.

–*Wordsworth*

The next morning Robin Hood convened his foresters, and desired Little John, for the baron's edification, to read over the laws of their forest society. Little John read aloud with a stentorophonic voice.

"At a high court of foresters, held under the greenwood tree, an hour after sun-rise, Robin Hood President, William Scarlet Vice-President, Little John Secretary: the following articles, moved by Friar Tuck in his capacity of Peer Spiritual, and seconded by Much the Miller, were unanimously agreed to.

"The principles of our society are six: Legitimacy, Equity, Hospitality, Chivalry, Chastity, and Courtesy.

"The articles of Legitimacy are four:

"I. Our government is legitimate, and our society is founded on the one golden rule of right, consecrated by the universal consent of mankind, and by the practice of all ages, individuals, and nations: namely, To keep what we have, and to catch what we can.

"II. Our government being legitimate, all our proceedings shall be legitimate: wherefore we declare war against the whole world, and every forester is by this legitimate declaration legitimately invested with a roving commission, to make lawful prize of every thing that comes in his way.

"III. All forest laws but our own we declare to be null and void.

"IV. All such of the old laws of England as do not in any way interfere with, or militate against, the views of this honourable assembly, we will loyally adhere to and maintain. The rest we declare null and void as far as relates to ourselves, in all cases wherein a vigour beyond the law may be conducive to our own interest and preservation."

"The articles of Equity are three:

"I. The balance of power among the people being very much deranged, by one having too much and another nothing, we hereby resolve ourselves into a congress or court of equity, to restore as far as in us lies the said natural balance of power, by taking from all who have too much as much of the said too much as we can lay our hands on; and giving to those who have nothing such a portion thereof as it may seem to us expedient to part with.

"II. In all cases a quorum of foresters shall constitute a court of equity, and as many as may be strong enough to manage the matter in hand shall constitute a quorum.

"III. All usurers, monks, courtiers, and other drones of the great hive of society, who shall be found laden with any portion of the honey whereof they have wrongfully despoiled the industrious bee, shall be rightfully despoiled thereof in turn; and all bishops and abbots shall be bound and beaten, [5]especially the abbot of Doncaster; as shall also all sheriffs, especially the sheriff of Nottingham.

---

[5] says Robin Hood, in an old ballad. Perhaps, however, thus is to be taken not in a literal, but in a figurative sense from the binding and beating of wheat: for as all rich men were Robin's harvest, the bishops and archbishops must have been the finest and fattest ears among them, from which Robin merely proposes to thresh the grain when he directs them to be bound and beaten: and as Pharaoh's fat kine were typical of fat ears of wheat, so may fat ears of wheat, mutatis mutandis, be typical of fat kine.

"The articles of Hospitality are two:

"I. Postmen, carriers and market-folk, peasants and mechanics, farmers and millers, shall pass through our forest dominions without let or molestation.

"II. All other travellers through the forest shall be graciously invited to partake of Robin's hospitality; and if they come not willingly they shall be compelled; and the rich man shall pay well for his fare; and the poor man shall feast scot free, and peradventure receive bounty in proportion to his desert and necessity.

"The article of Chivalry is one:

"I. Every forester shall, to the extent of his power, aid and protect maids, widows, and orphans, and all weak and distressed persons whomsoever: and no woman shall be impeded or molested in any way; nor shall any company receive harm which any woman is in.

"The article of Chastity is one:

"I. Every forester, being Diana's forester and minion of the moon, shall commend himself to the grace of the Virgin, and shall have the gift of continency on pain of expulsion: that the article of chivalry may be secure from infringement, and maids, wives, and widows pass without fear through the forest.

"The article of Courtesy is one:

"I. No one shall miscall a forester. He who calls Robin Robert of Huntingdon, or salutes him by any other title or designation whatsoever except plain Robin Hood; or who calls Marian Matilda Fitzwater, or salutes her by any other title or designation whatsoever except plain Maid Marian; and so of all others; shall for every such offence forfeit a mark, to be paid to the friar.

"And these articles we swear to keep as we are good men and true. Carried by acclamation. God save King Richard.

"LITTLE JOHN, Secretary."

"Excellent laws," said the baron: "excellent, by the holy rood. William of Normandy, with my great great grandfather Fierabras at his elbow, could not have made better. And now, sweet Mawd—"

"A fine, a fine," cried the friar, "a fine, by the article of courtesy."

"Od's life," said the baron, "shall I not call my own daughter Mawd? Methinks there should be a special exception in my favour."

"It must not be," said Robin Hood: "our constitution admits no privilege."

"But I will commute," said the friar; "for twenty marks a year duly paid into my ghostly pocket you shall call your daughter Mawd two hundred times a day."

"Gramercy," said the baron, "and I agree, honest friar, when I can get twenty marks to pay: for till Prince John be beaten from Nottingham, my rents are like to prove but scanty."

"I will trust," said the friar, "and thus let us ratify the stipulation; so shall our laws and your infringement run together in an amicable parallel."

"But," said Little John, "this is a bad precedent, master friar. It is turning discipline into profit, penalty into perquisite, public justice into private revenue. It is rank corruption, master friar."

"Why are laws made?" said the friar. "For the profit of somebody. Of whom? Of him who makes them first, and of others as it may happen. Was not I legislator in the last article, and shall I not thrive by my own law?"

"Well then, sweet Mawd," said the baron, "I must leave you, Mawd: your life is very well for the young and the hearty, but it squares not with my age or my humour. I must house, Mawd. I must find refuge: but where? That is the question."

"Where Sir Guy of Gamwell has found it," said Robin Hood, "near the borders of Barnsdale. There you may dwell in safety with him and fair Alice, till King Richard return, and Little John shall give you safe conduct. You will have need to travel with caution, in disguise and without attendants, for Prince John commands all this vicinity, and will doubtless lay the country for you and Marian. Now it is first expedient to dismiss your retainers. If there be any among them who like our life, they may stay with us in the greenwood; the rest may return to their homes."

Some of the baron's men resolved to remain with Robin and Marian, and were furnished accordingly with suits of green, of which Robin always kept good store.

Marian now declared that as there was danger in the way to Barnsdale, she would accompany Little John and the baron, as she should not be happy unless she herself saw her father placed in security. Robin was very unwilling to consent to this, and assured her that there was more danger for her than the baron: but Marian was absolute.

"If so, then," said Robin, "I shall be your guide instead of Little John, and I shall leave him and Scarlet joint-regents of Sherwood during my absence, and the voice of Friar Tuck shall be decisive between them if they differ in nice questions of state policy." Marian objected to this, that there was more danger for Robin than either herself or the baron: but Robin was absolute in his turn.

"Talk not of my voice," said the friar; "for if Marian be a damsel errant, I will be her ghostly esquire."

Robin insisted that this should not be, for number would only expose them to greater risk of detection. The friar, after some debate, reluctantly acquiesced.

While they were discussing these matters, they heard the distant sound of horses' feet.

"Go," said Robin to Little John, "and invite yonder horseman to dinner."

Little John bounded away, and soon came before a young man, who was riding in a melancholy manner, with the bridle hanging loose on the horse's neck, and his eyes drooping towards the ground.

"Whither go you?" said Little John.

"Whithersoever my horse pleases," said the young man.

"And that shall be," said Little John, "whither I please to lead him. I am commissioned to invite you to dine with my master."

"Who is your master?" said the young man.

"Robin Hood," said Little John.

"The bold outlaw?" said the stranger. "Neither he nor you should have made me turn an inch aside yesterday; but to-day I care not."

"Then it is better for you," said Little John, "that you came to-day than yesterday, if you love dining in a whole skin: for my master is the pink of courtesy: but if his guests prove stubborn, he bastes them and his venison together, while the friar says mass before meat."

The young man made no answer, and scarcely seemed to hear what Little John was saying, who therefore took the horse's bridle and led him to where Robin and his foresters were setting forth their dinner. Robin seated the young man next to Marian. Recovering a little from his stupor, he looked with much amazement at her, and the baron, and Robin, and the friar; listened to their conversation, and seemed much astonished to find himself in such holy and courtly company. Robin helped him largely to rumble-pie and cygnet and pheasant, and the other dainties of his table; and the friar pledged him in ale and wine, and exhorted him to make good cheer. But the young man drank little, ate less, spake nothing, and every now and then sighed heavily.

When the repast was ended, "Now," said Robin, "you are at liberty to pursue your journey: but first be pleased to pay for your dinner."

"That would I gladly do, Robin," said the young man, "but all I have about me are five shillings and a ring. To the five shillings you shall be welcome, but for the ring I will fight while there is a drop of blood in my veins."

"Gallantly spoken," said Robin Hood. "A love-token, without doubt: but you must submit to our forest laws. Little John must search; and if he find no more than you say, not a penny will I touch; but if you have spoken false, the whole is forfeit to our fraternity."

"And with reason," said the friar; "for thereby is the truth maintained The abbot of Doubleflask swore there was no money in his valise, and Little John forthwith emptied it of four hundred pounds. Thus was the abbot's perjury but of one minute's duration; for though his speech was false in the utterance, yet was it no sooner uttered than it became true, and we should have been participes criminis to have suffered the holy abbot to depart in falsehood: whereas he came to us a false priest, and we sent him away a true man. Marry, we turned his cloak to further account, and thereby hangs a tale that may be either said or sung; for in truth I am minstrel here as well as chaplain; I pray for good success to our just and necessary warfare, and sing thanks-giving odes when our foresters bring in booty:

Bold Robin has robed him in ghostly attire,
And forth he is gone like a holy friar,
Singing, hey down, ho down, down, derry down:
And of two grey friars he soon was aware,
Regaling themselves with dainty fare,
All on the fallen leaves so brown.

"Good morrow, good brothers," said bold Robin
Hood, "And what make you in the good greenwood,
Singing hey down, ho down, down, derry down!
Now give me, I pray you, wine and food;
For none can I find in the good greenwood,
All on the fallen leaves so brown."

"Good brother," they said, "we would give you full fain,
But we have no more than enough for twain,
Singing, hey down, ho down, down, derry down."
"Then give me some money," said bold Robin Hood,
"For none can I find in the good greenwood,
All on the fallen leaves so brown."

"No money have we, good brother," said they:
"Then," said he, "we three for money will pray:
Singing, hey down, ho down, down, derry down:
And whatever shall come at the end of our prayer,
We three holy friars will piously share,
All on the fallen leaves so brown."

"We will not pray with thee, good brother, God wot:
For truly, good brother, thou pleasest us not,
Singing hey down, ho down, down, derry down:"
Then up they both started from Robin to run,
But down on their knees Robin pulled them each one,
All on the fallen leaves so brown.

The grey friars prayed with a doleful face,
But bold Robin prayed with a right merry grace,
Singing, hey down, ho down, down, derry down:
And when they had prayed, their portmanteau he took,
And from it a hundred good angels he shook,
All on the fallen leaves so brown.

"The saints," said bold Robin, "have hearkened our prayer,
And here's a good angel apiece for your share:
If more you would have, you must win ere you wear:

Singing hey down, ho down, down, derry down:"
Then he blew his good horn with a musical cheer,
And fifty green bowmen came trooping full near,
And away the grey friars they bounded like deer,
All on the fallen leaves so brown.

❖❖❖

Chapter–XIII

What can a young lassie, what shall a young lassie,
What can a young lassie do wi'an auld man?

—Burns

Here is but five shillings and a ring," said Little John, "and the young man has spoken true."

"Then," said Robin to the stranger, "if want of money be the cause of your melancholy, speak. Little John is my treasurer, and he shall disburse to you."

"It is, and it is not," said the stranger; "it is, because, had I not wanted money I had never lost my love; it is not, because, now that I have lost her, money would come too late to regain her."

"In what way have you lost her?" said Robin: "let us clearly know that she is past regaining, before we give up our wishes to restore her to you."

"She is to be married this day," said the stranger, "and perhaps is married by this, to a rich old knight; and yesterday I knew it not."

"What is your name?" said Robin.

"Allen," said the stranger.

"And where is the marriage to take place, Allen?" said Robin.

"At Edwinstow church," said Allen, "by the bishop of Nottingham."

"I know that bishop," said Robin; "he dined with me a month since, and paid three hundred pounds for his dinner. He has a good ear and loves music. The friar sang to him to some tune.

Give me my harper's cloak, and I will play a part at this wedding.

"These are dangerous times, Robin," said Marian, "for playing pranks out of the forest."

"Fear not," said Robin; "Edwinstow lies not Nottingham-ward, and I will take my precautions."

Robin put on his harper's cloak, while Little John painted his eyebrows and cheeks, tipped his nose with red, and tied him on a comely beard. Marian confessed, that had she not been present at the metamorphosis, she should not have known her own true Robin. Robin took his harp and went to the wedding.

Robin found the bishop and his train in the church porch, impatiently expecting the arrival of the bride and bridegroom. The clerk was observing to the bishop that the knight was somewhat gouty, and that the necessity of walking the last quarter of a mile from the road to the churchyard probably detained the lively bridegroom rather longer than had been calculated upon.

"Oh! by my fey," said the music-loving bishop, "here comes a harper in the nick of time, and now I care not how long they tarry. Ho! honest friend, are you come to play at the wedding?"

"I am come to play anywhere," answered Robin, "where I can get a cup of sack; for which I will sing the praise of the donor in lofty verse, and emblazon him with any virtue which he may wish to have the credit of possessing, without the trouble of practising.

"A most courtly harper," said the bishop; "I will fill thee with sack; I will make thee a walking butt of sack, if thou wilt delight my ears with thy melodies."

"That will I," said Robin; "in what branch of my art shall I exert my faculty? I am passing well in all, from the anthem to the glee, and from the dirge to the coranto."

"It would be idle," said the bishop, "to give thee sack for playing me anthems, seeing that I myself do receive sack for hearing them sung. Therefore, as the occasion is festive, thou shalt play me a coranto."

Robin struck up and played away merrily, the bishop all the while in great delight, noddling his head, and beating time with his foot, till the bride and bridegroom appeared. The bridegroom was richly apparelled, and came slowly and painfully forward, hobbling and leering, and pursing up his mouth into a smile of resolute defiance to the gout, and of tender complacency towards his lady love, who, shining like gold at the old knight's expense, followed slowly between her father and mother, her cheeks pale, her head drooping, her steps faltering, and her eyes reddened with tears.

Robin stopped his minstrelsy, and said to the bishop, "This seems to me an unfit match."

"What do you say, rascal?" said the old knight, hobbling up to him.

"I say," said Robin, "this seems to me an unfit match. What, in the devil's name, can you want with a young wife, who have one foot in flannels and the other in the grave?"

"What is that to thee, sirrah varlet?" said the old knight; "stand away from the porch, or I will fracture thy sconce with my cane."

"I will not stand away from the porch," said Robin, "unless the bride bid me, and tell me that you are her own true love."

"Speak," said the bride's father, in a severe tone, and with a look of significant menace. The girl looked alternately at her father and Robin. She attempted to speak, but her voice failed in the effort, and she burst into tears.

"Here is lawful cause and just impediment," said Robin, "and I forbid the banns."

"Who are you, villain?" said the old knight, stamping his sound foot with rage.

"I am the Roman law," said Robin, "which says that there shall not be more than ten years between a man and his wife; and here are five times ten: and so says the law of nature."

"Honest harper," said the bishop, "you are somewhat over-officious here, and less courtly than I deemed you. If you love sack, forbear; for this course will never bring you a drop. As to your Roman law, and your law of nature, what right have they to say any thing which the law of Holy Writ says not?"

"The law of Holy Writ does say it," said Robin; "I expound it so to say; and I will produce sixty commentators to establish my exposition."

And so saying, he produced a horn from beneath his cloak, and blew three blasts, and threescore bowmen in green came leaping from the bushes and trees; and young Allen was the first among them to give Robin his sword, while Friar Tuck and Little John marched up to the altar. Robin stripped the bishop and clerk of their robes, and put them on the friar and Little John; and Allen advanced to take the hand of the bride. Her cheeks grew red and her eyes grew bright, as she locked her hand in her lover's, and tripped lightly with him into the church.

"This marriage will not stand," said the bishop, "for they have not been thrice asked in church."

"We will ask them seven times," said Little John, "lest three should not suffice."

"And in the meantime," said Robin, "the knight and the bishop shall dance to my harping."

So Robin sat in the church porch and played away merrily, while his foresters formed a ring, in the centre of which the knight and bishop danced with exemplary alacrity; and if they relaxed their exertions, Scarlet gently touched them up with the point of an arrow.

The knight grimaced ruefully, and begged Robin to think of his gout.

"So I do," said Robin; "this is the true antipodagron: you shall dance the gout away, and be thankful to me while you live. I told you," he added to the bishop, "I would play at this wedding; but you did not tell me that you would dance at it. The next couple you marry, think of the Roman law."

The bishop was too much out of breath to reply; and now the young couple issued from church, and the bride having made a farewell obeisance to her parents, they departed together with the foresters, the parents storming, the attendants laughing, the bishop puffing and blowing, and the knight rubbing his gouty foot, and uttering doleful lamentations for the gold and jewels with which he had so unwittingly adorned and cowered the bride.

Chapter–XIV

As ye came from the holy land
Of blessed Walsinghame,
Oh met ye not with my true love,
As by the way ye came?

–Old Ballad

In pursuance of the arrangement recorded in the twelfth chapter, the baron, Robin, and Marian disguised themselves as pilgrims returned from Palestine, and travelling from the sea-coast of Hampshire to their home in Northumberland. By dint of staff and cockle-shell, sandal and scrip, they proceeded in safety the greater part of the way (for Robin had many sly inns and resting-places between Barnsdale and Sherwood), and were already on the borders of Yorkshire, when, one evening, they passed within view of a castle, where they saw a lady standing on a turret, and surveying the whole extent of the valley through which they were passing. A servant came running from the castle, and delivered to them a message from his lady, who was sick with expectation of news from her lord in the Holy Land, and entreated them to come to her, that she might question them concerning him. This was an awkward occurrence: but there was no presence for refusal, and they followed the servant into the castle. The baron, who had been in Palestine in his youth, undertook to be spokesman on the occasion, and to relate his own adventures to the lady as having happened to the lord in question. This preparation enabled him to be so minute and circumstantial in his detail, and so coherent in his replies to her questions, that the lady fell implicitly into the delusion, and was delighted to find that her lord was alive and in health, and in high favour with the king, and performing prodigies of valour in the name of his lady, whose miniature he always wore in his bosom. The baron guessed at this circumstance from the customs of that age, and happened to be in the right.

"This miniature," added the baron, "I have had the felicity to see, and should have known you by it among a million." The baron was a little embarrassed by some questions of the lady concerning her lord's personal appearance; but Robin came to his aid, observing a picture suspended opposite to him on the wall, which he made a bold conjecture to be that of the lord in question; and making a calculation of the influences of time and war, which he weighed with a comparison of the lady's age, he gave a description of her lord sufficiently like the picture in its groundwork to be a true resemblance, and sufficiently differing from it in circumstances to be more an original than a copy. The lady was completely deceived, and entreated them to partake her hospitality for the night; but this they deemed it prudent to decline, and with many humble thanks for her kindness, and representations of the necessity of not delaying their homeward course, they proceeded on their way.

As they passed over the drawbridge, they met Sir Ralph Montfaucon and his squire, who were wandering in quest of Marian, and were entering to claim that hospitality which the pilgrims had declined. Their countenances struck Sir Ralph with a kind of imperfect recognition, which would never have been matured, but that the eyes of Marian, as she passed him, encountered his, and the images of those stars of beauty continued involuntarily twinkling in his sensorium to the exclusion of all other ideas, till memory, love, and hope concurred with imagination to furnish a probable reason for their haunting him so pertinaciously. Those eyes, he thought, were certainly the eyes of Matilda Fitzwater; and if the eyes were hers, it was extremely probable, if not logically consecutive, that the rest of the body they belonged to was hers also. Now, if it were really Matilda Fitzwater, who were her two companions? The baron? Aye, and the elder pilgrim was something like him. And the earl of Huntingdon? Very probably. The earl and the baron might be good friends again, now that they were both in disgrace together. While he was revolving these cogitations, he was introduced to the lady, and after claiming and receiving the promise of hospitality, he inquired what she knew of the pilgrims who had just departed? The lady told him they were newly returned from Palestine, having been long in the Holy Land. The knight expressed some scepticism on this point. The lady replied, that they had given her so minute a detail of her lord's proceedings, and so accurate a description of his person, that she could not be deceived in them. This staggered the knight's confidence in his own penetration; and if it had not been a heresy in knighthood to suppose for a moment that there could be in rerum natura such another pair of eyes as those of his mistress, he would have acquiesced implicitly in the lady's judgment. But while the lady and the knight were conversing, the warder blew his bugle-horn, and presently entered a confidential messenger from Palestine, who gave her to understand that her lord was well; but entered into a detail of his adventures most completely at variance with the baron's narrative, to which not the correspondence of a single incident gave the remotest colouring of similarity. It now became manifest that the pilgrims were not true men; and Sir Ralph Montfaucon sate down to supper with his head full of cogitations, which we shall leave him to chew and digest with his pheasant and canary.

Meanwhile our three pilgrims proceeded on their way. The evening set in black and lowering, when Robin turned aside from the main track, to seek an asylum for the night, along a narrow way that led between rocky and woody hills. A peasant observed the pilgrims as they entered that narrow pass, and called after them: "Whither go you, my masters? there are rogues in that direction."

"Can you show us a direction," said Robin, "in which there are none? If so we will take it in preference." The peasant grinned, and walked away whistling.

The pass widened as they advanced, and the woods grew thicker and darker around them. Their path wound along the slope of a woody declivity, which rose high above them in a thick rampart of foliage, and descended almost precipitously to the bed of a small river, which they heard dashing in its rocky channel, and saw its white foam gleaming at intervals in the last faint glimmerings of twilight. In a short time all was dark, and the rising voice of the wind foretold a coming storm. They turned a point of the valley, and saw a light below them in the depth of the hollow, shining through a cottage-casement and dancing in its reflection on the restless stream. Robin blew his horn, which was answered from below. The cottage door opened: a boy came forth with a torch, ascended the steep, showed tokens of great delight at meeting with Robin, and lighted them down a flight of steps rudely cut in the rock, and over a series of rugged stepping-stones, that crossed the channel of the river. They entered the cottage, which exhibited neatness, comfort, and plenty, being amply enriched with pots, pans, and pipkins, and adorned with flitches of bacon and sundry similar ornaments, that gave goodly promise in the firelight that gleamed upon the rafters. A woman, who seemed just old enough to be the boy's mother, had thrown down her spinning wheel in her joy at the sound of Robin's horn, and was bustling with singular alacrity to set forth her festal ware and prepare an abundant supper. Her features, though not beautiful, were agreeable and expressive, and were now lighted up with such manifest joy at the sight of Robin, that Marian could not help feeling a momentary touch of jealousy, and a half-formed suspicion that Robin had broken his forest law, and had occasionally gone out of bounds, as other great men have done upon occasion, in order to reconcile the breach of the spirit, with the preservation of the letter, of their own legislation. However, this suspicion, if it could be said to exist in a mind so generous as Marian's, was very soon dissipated by the entrance of the woman's husband, who testified as much joy as his wife had done at the sight of Robin; and in a short time the whole of the party were amicably seated round a smoking supper of river-fish and wild wood fowl, on which the baron fell with as much alacrity as if he had been a true pilgrim from Palcstine.

The husband produced some recondite flasks of wine, which were laid by in a binn consecrated to Robin, whose occasional visits to them in his wanderings were the festal days of these warm-hearted cottagers, whose manners showed that they had not been born to this low estate. Their story had no mystery, and Marian easily collected it from the tenour of their conversation. The young man had been, like Robin, the victim of an usurious abbot, and had been outlawed for debt, and his nut-brown maid had accompanied him to the depths of Sherwood, where they lived an unholy and illegitimate life, killing the king's deer, and never hearing mass. In this state, Robin, then earl of Huntingdon, discovered them in one of his huntings, and gave them aid and protection. When Robin himself became an outlaw, the necessary qualification or gift of continency was too hard a law for our lovers to subscribe to; and as they were thus disqualified for foresters, Robin had found them a retreat in this romantic and secluded spot. He had done similar service to other lovers similarly circumstanced, and had disposed them in various wild scenes which he and his men had discovered in their flittings from place to place, supplying them with all necessaries and comforts from the reluctant disgorgings of fat abbots and usurers. The benefit was in some measure mutual; for these cottages served him as resting-places in his removals, and enabled him to travel untraced and unmolested; and in the delight with which he was always received he found himself even more welcome than he would have been at an inn; and this is saying very much for gratitude and affection together. The smiles which surrounded him were of his own creation, and he participated in the happiness he had bestowed.

The casements began to rattle in the wind, and the rain to beat upon the windows. The wind swelled to a hurricane, and the rain dashed like a flood against the glass. The boy retired to his little bed, the wife trimmed the lamp, the husband heaped logs upon the fire: Robin broached another flask; and Marian filled the baron's cup, and sweetened Robin's by touching its edge with her lips.

"Well," said the baron, "give me a roof over my head, be it never so humble. Your greenwood canopy is pretty and pleasant in sunshine; but if I were doomed to live under it, I should wish it were water-tight."

"But," said Robin, "we have tents and caves for foul weather, good store of wine and venison, and fuel in abundance."

"Ay, but," said the baron, "I like to pull off my boots of a night, which you foresters seldom do, and to ensconce myself thereafter in a comfortable bed. Your beech-root is over-hard for a couch, and your mossy stump is somewhat rough for a bolster."

"Had you not dry leaves," said Robin, "with a bishop's surplice over them? What would you have softer? And had you not an abbot's travelling cloak for a coverlet? What would you have warmer?"

"Very true," said the baron, "but that was an indulgence to a guest, and I dreamed all night of the sheriff of Nottingham. I like to feel myself safe," he added, stretching out his legs to the fire, and throwing himself back in his chair with the air of a man determined to be comfortable. "I like to feel myself safe," said the baron.

At that moment the woman caught her husband's arm, and all the party following the direction of her eyes, looked simultaneously to the window, where they had just time to catch a glimpse of an apparition of an armed head, with its plumage tossing in the storm, on which the light shone from within, and which disappeared immediately.

Chapter–XV

O knight, thou lack'st a cup of canary.
When did I see thee so put down?

–Twelfth Night

Several knocks, as from the knuckles of an iron glove, were given to the door of the cottage, and a voice was heard entreating shelter from the storm for a traveller who had lost his way. Robin arose and went to the door.

"What are you?" said Robin.

"A soldier," replied the voice: "an unfortunate adherent of Longchamp, flying the vengeance of Prince John."

"Are you alone?" said Robin.

"Yes," said the voice: "it is a dreadful night. Hospitable cottagers, pray give me admittance. I would not have asked it but for the storm. I would have kept my watch in the woods."

"That I believe," said Robin. "You did not reckon on the storm when you turned into this pass. Do you know there are rogues this way?"

"I do," said the voice.

"So do I," said Robin.

A pause ensued, during which Robin listening attentively caught a faint sound of whispering.

"You are not alone," said Robin. "Who are your companions?"

"None but the wind and the water," said the voice, "and I would I had them not."

"The wind and the water have many voices," said Robin, "but I never before heard them say, What shall we do?"

Another pause ensued: after which,

"Look ye, master cottager," said the voice, in an altered tone, "if you do not let us in willingly, we will break down the door."

"Ho! ho!" roared the baron, "you are become plural are you, rascals? How many are there of you, thieves? What, I warrant, you thought to rob and murder a poor harmless cottager and his wife, and did not dream of a garrison? You looked for no weapon of opposition but spit, poker, and basting ladle, wielded by unskilful hands: but, rascals, here is short sword and long cudgel in hands well tried in war, wherewith you shall be drilled into cullenders and beaten into mummy."

No reply was made, but furious strokes from without resounded upon the door. Robin, Marian, and the baron threw by their pilgrim's attire, and stood in arms on the defensive. They were provided with swords, and the cottager gave them bucklers and helmets, for all Robin's haunts were furnished with secret armouries. But they kept their swords sheathed, and the baron wielded a ponderous spear, which he pointed towards the door ready to run through the first that should enter, and Robin and Marian each held a bow with the arrow drawn to its head and pointed in the same direction. The cottager flourished a strong cudgel (a weapon in the use of which he prided himself on being particularly expert), and the wife seized the spit from the fireplace, and held it as she saw the baron hold his spear. The storm of wind and rain continued to beat on the roof and the casement, and the storm of blows to resound upon the door, which at length gave way with a violent crash, and a cluster of armed men appeared without, seemingly not less than twelve. Behind them rolled the stream now changed from a gentle and shallow river to a mighty and impetuous torrent, roaring in waves of yellow foam, partially reddened by the light that streamed through the open door, and turning up its convulsed surface in flashes of shifting radiance from restless masses of half-visible shadow. The stepping-stones, by which the intruders must have crossed, were buried under the waters. On the opposite bank the light fell on the stems and boughs of the rock-rooted oak and ash tossing and swaying in the blast, and sweeping the flashing spray with their leaves.

The instant the door broke, Robin and Marian loosed their arrows. Robin's arrow struck one of the assailants in the juncture of the shoulder, and disabled his right arm: Marian's struck a second in the juncture of the knee, and rendered him unserviceable; for the night. The baron's long spear struck on the mailed breastplate of a third, and being stretched to its full extent by the long-armed hero, drove him to the edge of the torrent, and plunged him into its eddies, along which he was whirled down the darkness of the descending stream, calling vainly on his comrades for aid, till his voice was lost in the mingled roar of the waters and the wind. A fourth springing through the door was laid prostrate by the cottager's cudgel: but the wife being less dexterous than her company, though an Amazon in strength, missed her pass at a fifth, and drove the point of the spit several inches into the right hand door-post as she stood close to the left, and thus made a new barrier which the invaders could not pass without dipping under it and submitting their necks to the sword: but one of the assailants seizing it with gigantic rage, shook it at once from the grasp of its holder and from its lodgment in the post, and at the same time made good the irruption of the rest of his party into the cottage.

Now raged an unequal combat, for the assailants fell two to one on Robin, Marian, the baron, and the cottager; while the wife, being deprived of her spit, converted every thing that was at hand to a missile, and rained pots, pans, and pipkins on the armed heads of the enemy. The baron raged like a tiger, and the cottager laid about him like a thresher. One of the soldiers struck Robin's sword from his hand and brought him on his knee, when the boy, who had been roused by the tumult and had been peeping through the inner door, leaped forward in his shirt, picked up the sword and replaced it in Robin's hand, who instantly springing up, disarmed and wounded one of his antagonists, while the other was laid prostrate under the dint of a brass cauldron launched by the Amazonian dame. Robin now turned to the aid of Marian, who was parrying most dexterously the cuts and slashes of her two assailants, of whom Robin delivered her from one, while a well-applied blow of her sword struck off the helmet of the other, who fell on his knees to beg a boon, and she recognised Sir Ralph Montfaucon. The men who were engaged with the baron and the peasant, seeing their leader subdued, immediately laid down their arms and cried for quarter. The wife brought some strong rope, and the baron tied their arms behind them.

"Now, Sir Ralph," said Marian, "once more you are at my mercy."

"That I always am, cruel beauty," said the discomfited lover.

"Odso! courteous knight," said the baron, "is this the return you make for my beef and canary, when you kissed my daughter's hand in token of contrition for your intermeddling at her wedding? Heart, I am glad to see she has given you a bloody coxcomb. Slice him down, Mawd! slice him down, and fling him into the river."

"Confess," said Marian, "what brought you here, and how did you trace our steps?"

"I will confess nothing," said the knight.

"Then confess you, rascal," said the baron, holding his sword to the throat of the captive squire.

"Take away the sword," said the squire, "it is too near my mouth, and my voice will not come out for fear: take away the sword, and I will confess all." The baron dropped his sword, and the squire proceeded; "Sir Ralph met you, as you quitted Lady Falkland's castle, and by representing to her who you were, borrowed from her such a number of her retainers as he deemed must ensure your capture, seeing that your familiar the friar was not at your elbow. We set forth without delay, and traced you first by means of a peasant who saw you turn into this valley, and afterwards by the light from the casement of this solitary dwelling. Our design was to have laid an ambush for you in the morning, but the storm and your observation of my unlucky face through the casement made us change our purpose; and what followed you can tell better than I can, being indeed masters of the subject."

"You are a merry knave," said the baron, "and here is a cup of wine for you."

"Gramercy," said the squire, "and better late than never: but I lacked a cup of this before. Had I been pot-valiant, I had held you play."

"Sir knight," said Marian, "this is the third time you have sought the life of my lord and of me, for mine is interwoven with his. And do you think me so spiritless as to believe that I can be yours by compulsion? Tempt me not again, for the next time shall be the last, and the fish of the nearest river shall commute the flesh of a recreant knight into the fast-day dinner of an uncarnivorous friar. I spare you now, not in pity but in scorn. Yet shall you swear to a convention never more to pursue or molest my lord or me, and on this condition you shall live."

The knight had no alternative but to comply, and swore, on the honour of knighthood, to keep the convention inviolate. How well he kept his oath we shall have no opportunity of narrating: Di lui la nostra istoria piu non parla.

❖❖❖

Chapter–XVI

Carry me over the water, thou fine fellowe.

—Old Ballad

The pilgrims, without experiencing further molestation, arrived at the retreat of Sir Guy of Gamwell. They found the old knight a cup too low; partly from being cut off from the scenes of his old hospitality and the shouts of his Nottinghamshire vassals, who were wont to make the rafters of his ancient hall re-echo to their revelry; but principally from being parted from his son, who had long been the better half of his flask and pasty. The arrival of our visitors cheered him up; and finding that the baron was to remain with him, he testified his delight and the cordiality of his welcome by pegging him in the ribs till he made him roar.

Robin and Marian took an affectionate leave of the baron and the old knight; and before they quitted the vicinity of Barnsdale, deeming it prudent to return in a different disguise, they laid aside their pilgrim's attire, and assumed the habits and appurtenances of wandering minstrels.

They travelled in this character safely and pleasantly, till one evening at a late hour they arrived by the side of a river, where Robin looking out for a mode of passage perceived a ferry-boat safely moored in a nook on the opposite bank; near which a chimney sending up a wreath of smoke through the thick-set willows, was the only symptom of human habitation; and Robin naturally conceiving the said chimney and wreath of smoke to be the outward signs of the inward ferryman, shouted "Over!" with much strength and clearness; but no voice replied, and no ferryman appeared. Robin raised his voice, and shouted with redoubled energy, "Over, Over, O-o-o-over!" A faint echo alone responded "Over!" and again died away into deep silence: but after a brief interval a voice from among the willows, in a strange kind of mingled intonation that was half a shout and half a song, answered:

Over, over, over, jolly, jolly rover,Would you then come over? Over, over, over?Jolly, jolly rover, here's one lives in clover:
Who finds the clover? The jolly, jolly rover.
He finds the clover, let him then come over,
The jolly, jolly rover, over, over, over,

"I much doubt," said Marian, "if this ferryman do not mean by clover something more than the toll of his ferry-boat."

"I doubt not," answered Robin, "he is a levier of toll and tithe, which I shall put him upon proof of his right to receive, by making trial of his might to enforce."

The ferryman emerged from the willows and stepped into his boat. "As I live," exclaimed Robin, "the ferryman is a friar."

"With a sword," said Marian, "stuck in his rope girdle."

The friar pushed his boat off manfully, and was presently half over the river.

"It is friar Tuck," said Marian.

"He will scarcely know us," said Robin; "and if he do not, I will break a staff with him for sport."

The friar came singing across the water: the boat touched the land: Robin and Marian stepped on board: the friar pushed off again.

"Silken doublets, silken doublets," said the friar: "slenderly lined, I bow: your wandering minstrel is always poor toll: your sweet angels of voices pass current for a bed and a supper at the house of every lord that likes to hear the fame of his valour without the trouble of fighting for it. What need you of purse or pouch? You may sing before thieves. Pedlars, pedlars: wandering from door to door with the small ware of lies and cajolery: exploits for carpet-knights; honesty for courtiers; truth for monks, and chastity for nuns: a good saleable stock that costs the vender nothing, defies wear and tear, and when it has served a hundred customers is as plentiful and as marketable as ever. But, sirrahs, I'll none of your balderdash. You pass not hence without clink of brass, or I'll knock your musical noddles together till they ring like a pair of cymbals. That will be a new tune for your minstrelships."

This friendly speech of the friar ended as they stepped on the opposite bank. Robin had noticed as they passed that the summer stream was low.

"Why, thou brawling mongrel," said Robin, "that whether thou be thief, friar, or ferryman, or an ill-mixed compound of all three, passes conjecture, though I judge thee to be simple thief, what barkest thou at thus? Villain, there is clink of brass for thee. Dost thou see this coin? Dost thou hear this music? Look and listen: for touch thou shalt not: my minstrelship defies thee. Thou shalt carry me on thy back over the water, and receive nothing but a cracked sconce for thy trouble."

"A bargain," said the friar: "for the water is low, the labour is light, and the reward is alluring." And he stooped down for Robin, who mounted his back, and the friar waded with him over the river.

"Now, fine fellow," said the friar, "thou shalt carry me back over the water, and thou shalt have a cracked sconce for thy trouble."

Robin took the friar on his back, and waded with him into the middle of the river, when by a dexterous jerk he suddenly flung him off and plunged him horizontally over head and ears in the water. Robin waded to shore, and the friar, half swimming and half scrambling, followed.

"Fine fellow, fine fellow," said the friar, "now will I pay thee thy cracked sconce."

"Not so," said Robin, "I have not earned it: but thou hast earned it, and shalt have it."

It was not, even in those good old times, a sight of every day to see a troubadour and a friar playing at single-stick by the side of a river, each aiming with fell intent at the other's coxcomb. The parties were both so skilled in attack and defence, that their mutual efforts for a long time expended themselves in quick and loud rappings on each other's oaken staves. At length Robin by a dexterous feint contrived to score one on the friar's crown: but in the careless moment of triumph a splendid sweep of the friar's staff struck Robin's out of his hand into the middle of the river, and repaid his crack on the head with a degree of vigour that might have passed the bounds of a jest if Marian had not retarded its descent by catching the friar's arm.

"How now, recreant friar," said Marian; "what have you to say why you should not suffer instant execution, being detected in open rebellion against your liege lord? Therefore kneel down, traitor, and submit your neck to the sword of the offended law."

"Benefit of clergy," said the friar: "I plead my clergy. And is it you indeed, ye scapegraces? Ye are well disguised: I knew ye not, by my flask. Robin, jolly Robin, he buys a jest dearly that pays for it with a bloody coxcomb. But here is balm for all bruises, outward and inward. (The friar produced a flask of canary.) Wash thy wound twice and thy throat thrice with this solar concoction, and thou shalt marvel where was thy hurt. But what moved ye to this frolic? Knew ye not that ye could not appear in a mask more fashioned to move my bile than in that of these gilders and lackerers of the smooth surface of worthlessness, that bring the gold of true valour into disrepute, by stamping the baser metal with the fairer im-pression? I marvelled to find any such given to fighting (for they have an old instinct of self-preservation): but I rejoiced thereat, that I might discuss to them poetical justice: and therefore have I cracked thy sconce: for which, let this be thy medicine."

"But wherefore," said Marian, "do we find you here, when we left you joint lord warden of Sherwood?"

"I do but retire to my devotions," replied the friar. "This is my hermitage, in which I first took refuge when I escaped from my beloved brethren of Rubygill; and to which I still retreat at times from the vanities of the world, which else might cling to me too closely, since I have been promoted to be peer-spiritual of your forest-court. For, indeed, I do find in myself certain indications and admonitions that my day has past its noon; and none more cogent than this: that daily of bad wine I grow more intolerant, and of good wine have a keener and more fastidious relish. There is no surer symptom of receding years. The ferryman is my faithful varlet. I send him on some pious errand, that I may meditate in ghostly privacy, when my presence in the forest can best be spared: and when can it be better spared than now, seeing that the neighbourhood of Prince John, and his incessant perquisitions for Marian, have made the forest too hot to hold more of us than are needful to keep up a quorum, and preserve unbroken the continuity of our forest-dominion? For, in truth, without your greenwood majesties, we have hardly the wit to live in a body, and at the same time to keep our necks out of jeopardy, while that arch-rebel and traitor John infests the precincts of our territory."

The friar now conducted them to his peaceful cell, where he spread his frugal board with fish, venison, wild-fowl, fruit, and canary. Under the compound operation of this materia medica Robin's wounds healed apace, and the friar, who hated minstrelsy, began as usual chirping in his cups. Robin and

Marian chimed in with his tuneful humour till the midnight moon peeped in upon their revelry.

It was now the very witching time of night, when they heard a voice shouting, "Over!" They paused to listen, and the voice repeated "Over!" in accents clear and loud, but which at the same time either were in themselves, or seemed to be, from the place and the hour, singularly plaintive and dreary. The friar fidgetted about in his seat: fell into a deep musing: shook himself, and looked about him: first at Marian, then at Robin, then at Marian again; filled and tossed off a cup of canary, and relapsed into his reverie.

"Will you not bring your passenger over?" said Robin. The friar shook his head and looked mysterious.

"That passenger," said the friar, "will never come over. Every full moon, at midnight, that voice calls, 'Over!' I and my varlet have more than once obeyed the summons, and we have sometimes had a glimpse of a white figure under the opposite trees: but when the boat has touched the bank, nothing has been to be seen; and the voice has been heard no more till the midnight of the next full moon."

"It is very strange," said Robin.

"Wondrous strange," said the friar, looking solemn.

The voice again called "Over!" in a long plaintive musical cry.

"I must go to it," said the friar, "or it will give us no peace. I would all my customers were of this world. I begin to think that I am Charon, and that this river is Styx."

"I will go with you, friar," said Robin.

"By my flask," said the friar, "but you shall not."

"Then I will," said Marian.

"Still less," said the friar, hurrying out of the cell. Robin and Marian followed: but the friar outstepped them, and pushed off his boat.

A white figure was visible under the shade of the opposite trees. The boat approached the shore, and the figure glided away. The friar returned.

They re-entered the cottage, and sat some time conversing on the phenomenon they had seen. The friar sipped his wine, and after a time, said:

"There is a tradition of a damsel who was drowned here some years ago. The tradition is—"

But the friar could not narrate a plain tale: he therefore cleared his throat, and sang with due solemnity, in a ghostly voice:

A damsel came in midnight rain,
And called across the ferry:
The weary wight she called in vain,
Whose senses sleep did bury.
At evening, from her father's door
She turned to meet her lover:
At midnight, on the lonely shore,
She shouted "Over, over!"

She had not met him by the tree
Of their accustomed meeting,
And sad and sick at heart was she,
Her heart all wildly beating.
In chill suspense the hours went by,
The wild storm burst above her:
She turned her to the river nigh,
And shouted, "Over, over!"

A dim, discoloured, doubtful light
The moon's dark veil permitted,
And thick before her troubled sight
Fantastic shadows flitted.
Her lover's form appeared to glide,
And beckon o'er the water:
Alas! his blood that morn had dyed

Her brother's sword with slaughter.
Upon a little rock she stood,
To make her invocation:
She marked not that the rain-swoll'n flood
Was islanding her station.
The tempest mocked her feeble cry:
No saint his aid would give her:
The flood swelled high and yet more high,
And swept her down the river.

Yet oft beneath the pale moonlight,
When hollow winds are blowing,
The shadow of that maiden bright
Glides by the dark stream's flowing.
And when the storms of midnight rave,
While clouds the broad moon cover,
The wild gusts waft across the wave
The cry of, "Over, over!"

While the friar was singing, Marian was meditating: and when he had ended she said, "Honest friar, you have misplaced your tradition, which belongs to the aestuary of a nobler river, where the damsel was swept away by the rising of the tide, for which your land-flood is an indifferent substitute. But the true tradition of this stream I think I myself possess, and I will narrate it in your own way:

It was a friar of orders free,
A friar of Rubygill:
At the greenwood-tree a vow made he,
But he kept it very ill:
A vow made he of chastity,
But he kept it very ill.
He kept it, perchance, in the conscious shade
Of the bounds of the forest wherein it was made:
But he roamed where he listed, as free as the wind,
And he left his good vow in the forest behind:

For its woods out of sight were his vow out of mind,
With the friar of Rubygill.

In lonely hut himself he shut,
The friar of Rubygill;
Where the ghostly elf absolved himself,
To follow his own good will:
And he had no lack of canary sack,
To keep his conscience still.
And a damsel well knew, when at lonely midnight
It gleamed on the waters, his signal-lamp-light:
"Over! over!" she warbled with nightingale throat,
And the friar sprung forth at the magical note,
And she crossed the dark stream in his trim ferryboat,
With the friar of Rubygill."

"Look you now," said Robin, "if the friar does not blush. Many strange sights have I seen in my day, but never till this moment did I see a blushing friar."

"I think," said the friar, "you never saw one that blushed not, or you saw good canary thrown away. But you are welcome to laugh if it so please you. None shall laugh in my company, though it be at my expense, but I will have my share of the merriment. The world is a stage, and life is a farce, and he that laughs most has most profit of the performance. The worst thing is good enough to be laughed at, though it be good for nothing else; and the best thing, though it be good for something else, is good for nothing better."

And he struck up a song in praise of laughing and quaffing, without further adverting to Marian's insinuated accusation; being, perhaps, of opinion, that it was a subject on which the least said would be the soonest mended.

So passed the night. In the morning a forester came to the friar, with intelligence that Prince John had been compelled, by the urgency of his affairs in other quarters, to disembarrass

Nottingham Castle of his royal presence. Our wanderers returned joyfully to their forest-dominion, being thus relieved from the vicinity of any more formidable belligerent than their old bruised and beaten enemy the sheriff of Nottingham.

❖❖❖

Chapter–XVII

Oh! this life
Is nobler than attending for a check,
Richer than doing nothing for a bribe
Prouder than rustling in unpaid-for silk

– ***Cymbeline***

So Robin and Marian dwelt and reigned in the forest, ranging the glades and the greenwoods from the matins of the lark to the vespers of the nightingale, and administering natural justice according to Robin's ideas of rectifying the inequalities of human condition: raising genial dews from the bags of the rich and idle, and returning them in fertilising showers on the poor and industrious: an operation which more enlightened statesmen have happily reversed, to the unspeakable benefit of the community at large. The light footsteps of Marian were impressed on the morning dew beside the firmer step of her lover, and they shook its large drops about them as they cleared themselves a passage through the thick tall fern, without any fear of catching cold, which was not much in fashion in the twelfth century. Robin was as hospitable as Cathmor; for seven men stood on seven paths to call the stranger to his feast. It is true, he superadded the small improvement of making the stranger pay for it: than which what could be more generous? For Cathmor was himself the prime giver of his feast, whereas Robin was only the agent to a series of strangers, who provided in turn for the entertainment of their successors; which is carrying the disinterestedness of hospitality to its acme. Marian often killed the deer,

Which Scarlet dressed, and Friar Tuck blessed
While Little John wandered in search of a guest.

Robin was very devout, though there was great unity in his religion: it was exclusively given to our Lady the Virgin, and he never set forth in a morning till he had said three prayers, and had heard the sweet voice of his Marian singing a hymn to their mutual patroness. Each of his men had, as usual, a patron saint according to his name or taste. The friar chose a saint for himself, and fixed on Saint Botolph, whom he euphonised into Saint Bottle, and maintained that he was that very Panomphic Pantagruelian saint, well known in ancient France as a female divinity, by the name of La Dive Bouteille, whose oracular monosyllable "Trincq," is celebrated and under-stood by all nations, and is expounded by the learned doctor Alcofribas, [6]who has treated at large on the subject, to signify "drink." Saint Bottle, then, was the saint of Friar Tuck, who did not yield even to Robin and Marian in the assiduity of his devotions to his chosen patron. Such was their summer life, and in their winter caves they had sufficient furniture, ample provender, store of old wine, and assuredly no lack of fuel, with joyous music and pleasant discourse to charm away the season of darkness and storms.

The reader who desires to know more about this oracular divinity, may consult the said doctor Alcofribas Nasier, who will usher him into the adytum through the medium of the high priestess Bacbuc.

---

[6] Alcofribas Nasier: an anagram of Francois Rabelais, and his assumed appellation.

Many moons had waxed and waned, when on the afternoon of a lovely summer day a lusty broad-boned knight was riding through the forest of Sherwood. The sun shone brilliantly on the full green foliage, and afforded the knight a fine opportunity of observing picturesque effects, of which it is to be feared he did not avail himself. But he had not proceeded far, before he had an opportunity of observing something much more interesting, namely, a fine young outlaw leaning, in the true Sherwood fashion, with his back against a tree. The knight was preparing to ask the stranger a question, the answer to which, if correctly given, would have relieved him from a doubt that pressed heavily on his mind, as to whether he was in the right road or the wrong, when the youth prevented the inquiry by saying: "In God's name, sir knight, you are late to your meals. My master has tarried dinner for you these three hours."

"I doubt," said the knight, "I am not he you wot of. I am no where bidden to day and I know none in this vicinage."

"We feared," said the youth, "your memory would be treacherous: therefore am I stationed here to refresh it."

"Who is your master?" said the knight; "and where does he abide?"

"My master," said the youth, "is called Robin Hood, and he abides hard by."

"And what knows he of me?" said the knight.

"He knows you," answered the youth "as he does every way-faring knight and friar, by instinct."

"Gramercy," said the knight; "then I understand his bidding: but how if I say I will not come?"

"I am enjoined to bring you," said the youth. "If persuasion avail not, I must use other argument."

"Say'st thou so?" said the knight; "I doubt if thy stripling rhetoric would convince me."

"That," said the young forester, "we will see."

"We are not equally matched, boy," said the knight. "I should get less honour by thy conquest, than grief by thy injury."

"Perhaps," said the youth, "my strength is more than my seeming, and my cunning more than my strength. Therefore let it please your knighthood to dismount."

"It shall please my knighthood to chastise thy presumption," said the knight, springing from his saddle.

Hereupon, which in those days was usually the result of a meeting between any two persons anywhere, they proceeded to fight.

The knight had in an uncommon degree both strength and skill: the forester had less strength, but not less skill than the knight, and showed such a mastery of his weapon as reduced the latter to great admiration.

They had not fought many minutes by the forest clock, the sun; and had as yet done each other no worse injury than that the knight had wounded the forester's jerkin, and the forester had disabled the knight's plume; when they were interrupted by a voice from a thicket, exclaiming, "Well fought, girl: well fought. Mass, that had nigh been a shrewd hit. Thou owest him for that, lass. Marry, stand by, I'll pay him for thee."

The knight turning to the voice, beheld a tall friar issuing from the thicket, brandishing a ponderous cudgel.

"Who art thou?" said the knight.

"I am the church militant of Sherwood," answered the friar. "Why art thou in arms against our lady queen?"

"What meanest thou?" said the knight.

"Truly, this," said the friar, "is our liege lady of the forest, against whom I do apprehend thee in overt act of treason. What sayest thou for thyself?"

"I say," answered the knight, "that if this be indeed a lady, man never yet held me so long."

"Spoken," said the friar, "like one who hath done execution. Hast thou thy stomach full of steel? Wilt thou diversify thy repast with a taste of my oak-graff? Or wilt thou incline thine heart to our venison which truly is cooling? Wilt thou fight? or wilt thou dine? or wilt thou fight and dine? or wilt thou dine and fight? I am for thee, choose as thou mayest."

"I will dine," said the knight; "for with lady I never fought before, and with friar I never fought yet, and with neither will I ever fight knowingly: and if this be the queen of the forest, I will not, being in her own dominions, be backward to do her homage."

So saying, he kissed the hand of Marian, who was pleased most graciously to express her approbation.

"Gramercy, sir knight," said the friar, "I laud thee for thy courtesy, which I deem to be no less than thy valour. Now do thou follow me, while I follow my nose, which scents the pleasant odour of roast from the depth of the forest recesses. I will lead thy horse, and do thou lead my lady."

The knight took Marian's hand, and followed the friar, who walked before them, singing:

When the wind blows, when the wind blows
From where under buck the dry log glows,
What guide can you follow,
O'er brake and o'er hollow,
So true as a ghostly, ghostly nose?

❖❖❖

Chapter–XVIII

Robin and Richard were two pretty men.

—Mother Goose's Melody

They proceeded, following their infallible guide, first along a light elastic greensward under the shade of lofty and wide-spreading trees that skirted a sunny opening of the forest, then along labyrinthine paths, which the deer, the outlaw, or the woodman had made, through the close shoots of the young coppices, through the thick undergrowth of the ancient woods, through beds of gigantic fern that filled the narrow glades and waved their green feathery heads above the plume of the knight. Along these sylvan alleys they walked in single file; the friar singing and pioneering in the van, the horse plunging and floundering behind the friar, the lady following "in maiden meditation fancy free," and the knight bringing up the rear, much marvelling at the strange company into which his stars had thrown him. Their path had expanded sufficiently to allow the knight to take Marian's hand again, when they arrived in the august presence of Robin Hood and his court.

Robin's table was spread under a high overarching canopy of living boughs, on the edge of a natural lawn of verdure starred with flowers, through which a swift transparent rivulet ran sparkling in the sun. The board was covered with abundance of choice food and excellent liquor, not without the comeliness of snow-white linen and the splendour of costly plate, which the sheriff of Nottingham had unwillingly contributed to supply, at the same time with an excellent cook, whom Little John's art had spirited away to the forest with the contents of his master's silver scullery.

An hundred foresters were here assembled over-ready for their dinner, some seated at the table and some lying in groups under the trees.

Robin bade courteous welcome to the knight, who took his seat between Robin and Marian at the festal board; at which was already placed one strange guest in the person of a portly monk, sitting between Little John and Scarlet, with, his rotund physiognomy elongated into an unnatural oval by the conjoint influence of sorrow and fear: sorrow for the departed contents of his travelling treasury, a good-looking valise which was hanging empty on a bough; and fear for his personal safety, of which all the flasks and pasties before him could not give him assurance. The appearance of the knight, however, cheered him up with a semblance of protection, and gave him just sufficient courage to demolish a cygnet and a rumble-pie, which he diluted with the contents of two flasks of canary sack.

But wine, which sometimes creates and often increases joy, doth also, upon occasion, heighten sorrow: and so it fared now with our portly monk, who had no sooner explained away his portion of provender, than he began to weep and bewail himself bitterly.

"Why dost thou weep, man?" said Robin Hood. "Thou hast done thine embassy justly, and shalt have thy Lady's grace."

"Alack! alack!" said the monk: "no embassy had I, luckless sinner, as well thou wottest, but to take to my abbey in safety the treasure whereof thou hast despoiled me."

"Propound me his case," said Friar Tuck, "and I will give him ghostly counsel."

"You well remember," said Robin Hood, "the sorrowful knight who dined with us here twelve months and a day gone by."

"Well do I," said Friar Tuck. "His lands were in jeopardy with a certain abbot, who would allow him no longer day for their redemption. Whereupon you lent to him the four hundred pounds which he needed, and which he was to repay this day, though he had no better security to give than our Lady the Virgin."

"I never desired better," said Robin, "for she never yet failed to send me my pay; and here is one of her own flock, this faithful and well-favoured monk of St. Mary's, hath brought it me duly, principal and interest to a penny, as Little John can testify, who told it forth. To be sure, he denied having it, but that was to prove our faith. We sought and found it."

"I know nothing of your knight," said the monk: "and the money was our own, as the Virgin shall bless me."

"She shall bless thee," said Friar Tuck, "for a faithful messenger."

The monk resumed his wailing. Little John brought him his horse. Robin gave him leave to depart. He sprang with singular nimbleness into the saddle, and vanished without saying, God give you good day.

The stranger knight laughed heartily as the monk rode off.

"They say, sir knight," said Friar Tuck, "they should laugh who win: but thou laughest who art likely to lose."

"I have won," said the knight, "a good dinner, some mirth, and some knowledge: and I cannot lose by paying for them."

"Bravely said," answered Robin. "Still it becomes thee to pay: for it is not meet that a poor forester should treat a rich knight. How much money hast thou with thee?"

"Troth, I know not," said the knight. "Sometimes much, sometimes little, sometimes none. But search, and what thou findest, keep: and for the sake of thy kind heart and open hand, be it what it may, I shall wish it were more."

"Then, since thou sayest so," said Robin, "not a penny will I touch. Many a false churl comes hither, and disburses against his will: and till there is lack of these, I prey not on true men."

"Thou art thyself a true man, right well I judge, Robin," said the stranger knight, "and seemest more like one bred in court than to thy present outlaw life."

"Our life," said the friar, "is a craft, an art, and a mystery. How much of it, think you, could be learned at court?"

"Indeed, I cannot say," said the stranger knight: "but I should apprehend very little."

"And so should I," said the friar: "for we should find very little of our bold open practice, but should hear abundance of praise of our principles. To live in seeming fellowship and secret rivalry; to have a hand for all, and a heart for none; to be everybody's acquaintance, and nobody's friend; to meditate the ruin of all on whom we smile, and to dread the secret stratagems of all who smile on us; to pilfer honours and despoil fortunes, not by fighting in daylight, but by sapping in darkness: these are arts which the court can teach, but which we, by 'r Lady, have not learned. But let your court-minstrel tune up his throat to the praise of your court-hero, then come our principles into play: then is our practice extolled not by the same name, for their Richard is a hero, and our Robin is a thief: marry, your hero guts an exchequer, while your thief disembowels a portmanteau, your hero sacks a city, while your thief sacks a cellar: your hero marauds on a larger scale, and that is all the difference, for the principle and the virtue are one: but two of a trade cannot agree: therefore your hero makes laws to get rid of your thief, and gives him an ill name that he may hang him: for might is right, and the strong make laws for the weak, and they that make laws to serve their own turn do also make morals to give colour to their laws."

"Your comparison, friar," said the stranger, "fails in this: that your thief fights for profit, and your hero for honour. I have fought under the banners of Richard, and if, as you phrase it, he guts exchequers, and sacks cities, it is not to win treasure for himself, but to furnish forth the means of his greater and more glorious aim."

"Misconceive me not, sir knight," said the friar. "We all love and honour King Richard, and here is a deep draught to his health: but I would show you, that we foresters are miscalled by opprobrious names, and that our virtues, though they follow at humble distance, are yet truly akin to those of Coeur-de-Lion. I say not that Richard is a thief, but I say that Robin is a hero: and for honour, did ever yet man, miscalled thief, win greater honour than Robin? Do not all men grace him with some honourable epithet? The most gentle thief, the most courteous thief, the most bountiful thief, yea, and the most honest thief? Richard is courteous, bountiful, honest, and valiant: but so also is Robin: it is the false word that makes the unjust distinction. They are twin-spirits, and should be friends, but that fortune hath differently cast their lot: but their names shall descend together to the latest days, as the flower of their age and of England: for in the pure principles of freebootery have they excelled all men; and to the principles of freebootery, diversely developed, belong all the qualities to which song and story concede renown."

"And you may add, friar," said Marian, "that Robin, no less than Richard, is king in his own dominion; and that if his subjects be fewer, yet are they more uniformly loyal."

"I would, fair lady," said the stranger, "that thy latter observation were not so true. But I nothing doubt, Robin, that if Richard could hear your friar, and see you and your lady, as I now do, there is not a man in England whom he would take by the hand more cordially than yourself."

"Gramercy, sir knight," said Robin— But his speech was cut short by Little John calling, "Hark!"

All listened. A distant trampling of horses was heard. The sounds approached rapidly, and at length a group of horsemen glittering in holyday dresses was visible among the trees.

"God's my life!" said Robin, "what means this? To arms, my merrymen all."

"No arms, Robin," said the foremost horseman, riding up and springing from his saddle: "have you forgotten Sir William of the Lee?"

"No, by my fay," said Robin; "and right welcome again to Sherwood."

Little John bustled to re-array the disorganised economy of the table, and replace the dilapidations of the provender.

"I come late, Robin," said Sir William, "but I came by a wrestling, where I found a good yeoman wrongfully beset by a crowd of sturdy varlets, and I staid to do him right."

"I thank thee for that, in God's name," said Robin, "as if thy good service had been to myself."

"And here," said the knight, "is thy four hundred pound; and my men have brought thee an hundred bows and as many well-furnished quivers; which I beseech thee to receive and to use as a poor token of my grateful kindness to thee: for me and my wife and children didst thou redeem from beggary."

"Thy bows and arrows," said Robin, "will I joyfully receive: but of thy money, not a penny. It is paid already. My Lady, who was thy security, hath sent it me for thee."

Sir William pressed, but Robin was inflexible.

"It is paid," said Robin, "as this good knight can testify, who saw my Lady's messenger depart but now."

Sir William looked round to the stranger knight, and instantly fell on his knee, saying, "God save King Richard."

The foresters, friar and all, dropped on their knees together, and repeated in chorus: "God save King Richard."

"Rise, rise," said Richard, smiling: "Robin is king here, as his lady hath shown. I have heard much of thee, Robin, both of thy present and thy former state. And this, thy fair forest-queen, is, if tales say true, the lady Matilda Fitzwater."

Marian signed acknowledgment.

"Your father," said the king, "has approved his fidelity to me, by the loss of his lands, which the newness of my return, and many public cares, have not yet given me time to restore: but this justice shall be done to him, and to thee also, Robin, if thou wilt leave thy forest-life and resume thy earldom, and be a peer of Coeur-de-Lion: for braver heart and juster hand I never yet found."

Robin looked round on his men.

"Your followers," said the king, "shall have free pardon, and such of them as thou wilt part with shall have maintenance from me; and if ever I confess to priest, it shall be to thy friar."

"Gramercy to your majesty," said the friar; "and my inflictions shall be flasks of canary; and if the number be (as in grave cases I may, peradventure, make it) too great for one frail mortality, I will relieve you by vicarious penance, and pour down my own throat the redundancy of the burden."

Robin and his followers embraced the king's proposal. A joyful meeting soon followed with the baron and Sir Guy of Gamwell: and Richard himself honoured with his own presence a formal solemnization of the nuptials of our lovers, whom he constantly distinguished with his peculiar regard.

The friar could not say, Farewell to the forest, without something of a heavy heart: and he sang as he turned his back upon its bounds, occasionally reverting his head:

Ye woods, that oft at sultry noon
Have o'er me spread your messy shade:
Ye gushing streams, whose murmured tune
Has in my ear sweet music made,
While, where the dancing pebbles show
Deep in the restless fountain-pool
The gelid water's upward flow,
My second flask was laid to cool:

Ye pleasant sights of leaf and flower:
Ye pleasant sounds of bird and bee:
Ye sports of deer in sylvan bower:
Ye feasts beneath the greenwood tree:
Ye baskings in the vernal sun:
Ye slumbers in the summer dell:
Ye trophies that this arm has won:
And must ye hear your friar's farewell?

But the friar's farewell was not destined to be eternal. He was domiciled as the family confessor of the earl and countess of Huntingdon, who led a discreet and courtly life, and kept up old hospitality in all its munificence, till the death of King Richard and the usurpation of John, by placing their enemy in power, compelled them to return to their greenwood sovereignty; which, it is probable, they would have before done from choice, if their love of sylvan liberty had not been counteracted by their desire to retain the friendship of Coeur-de-Lion. Their old and tried adherents, the friar among the foremost, flocked again round their forest-banner; and in merry Sherwood they long lived together, the lady still retaining her former name of Maid Marian, though the appellation was then as much a misnomer as that of Little John.

❖❖❖❖❖❖